The Plant-Based Pair

Dining à Deux

Time Tamers

Time is a precious commodity, and let's face it: Nobody wants to come home to more work at the end of a long day. These recipes are designed with efficiency and flavor in mind, so you don't have to labor over a hot stove when you ought to be savoring a hot meal instead. With most meals clocking in at less than 30 minutes, you're left with time to enjoy life.

Waste Not, Want Not

We've all been there: Staring into the freezer, trying to decide which frost-covered container we'll dare to thaw out and possibly even eat—until we come to our senses and toss the mystery meal out. This collection of recipes is tailored for two, which helps you minimize waste and avoid Freezer-Burned Leftovers Syndrome.

Twice Is Nice

Paring down your recipes to serve two doesn't mean whittling down flavor. In this culinary collection, you'll discover bright flavors borrowed from different corners of the globe and wholesome goodness that tastes even better when devoured à deux. Think Creamy Truffled Linguini (page 119), Thai Peanut Slaw (page 51), and Sesame-Soba Noodle Soup (page 92) for a start!

Simply Delicious

Keeping it simple means relying on quality ingredients to make your supper (and breakfast, and lunch) sing. These recipes are built on a wholesome foundation of fresh ingredients that pack nutrition and flavor in every bite, and don't require you to complete a PhD in food science before breaking bread.

Healthy Helpings

These recipes not only taste good, but they're good for you, too. Healthy fats, great grains, and a plethora of freshly plucked produce mean more nutritional bang for your buck in every bite. From the Superb Sides & Alluring Appetizers straight through to Decadent Desserts, you can expect every mouthful to be delicious and nourishing.

THE Plant-Based Pair

A VEGAN COOKBOOK FOR TWO
WITH 125 PERFECTLY PORTIONED RECIPES

ROCKRIDGE
PRESS

Interior photo credits: Stockfood/Hilde Mèche, p.6; Stocksy/Emokė Szabo, p.7; Stockfood/Victoria Firmston, p.8; Shutterstock/Sergio Stakhnyk, p.12a; Shutterstock/Brent Hofacker, p.12b; Stocksy/Harald Walker, p.12c; Shutterstock/iravgustin, p.17a; Stocksy/Ina Peters, p.17b; Shutterstock/inacio pires, p.17c; Stockfood/People Pictures, p.18; Stockfood/Andrew Young, p.42; Stockfood/Harry Bischof, p.60; Stockfood/Gräfe & Unzer Verlag/mona binner PHOTOGRAPHIE, p.78; Stockfood/Gareth Morgans, p.96; Stockfood/People Pictures, p. 110; Stockfood/Gräfe & Unzer Verlag/Schütz, Anke, p.134; Stockfood/Tanya Zouev, p.148; Stockfood/Keller & Keller Photography, p.162; Stockfood/Ruth Küng

Cover photo credits: Front cover: Offset/Johnny Autry; back cover: StockFood/People Pictures, StockFood/Gräfe & Unzer Verlag/Mona Binner Photographie, StockFood/Victoria Firmston

Print ISBN: 978-1-62315-547-6 | e-Book ISBN: 978-1-62315-417-2

CONTENTS

INTRODUCTION

Few things in life are as satisfying as sitting down to a scrumptious meal and sharing the experience with a great dining companion. Add to that equation a colorful plate of tantalizing food that you've prepared yourselves, and the pleasure quotient takes a quantum leap. Every meal should be a special occasion where food is celebrated and relished in good company, and this cookbook is designed for home cooks who feel the same.

What sets this collection of recipes apart from the pack is that, in addition to being 100-percent delicious, each recipe is 100-percent vegan, and many of the recipes are also gluten-, soy-, and nut-free. The emphasis is on ease; ingredients will be easy to source at your local grocery store or natural-foods market, and portions are pared down to serve a duo of diners. More good news! Half the recipes take just 30 minutes or fewer to prepare. From Pad Thai with Tofu (page 121) to Garlicky Kale Crostini (page 62) and creamy Amaretto Mousse (page 144), you can expect oodles of wholesome flavor with a minimal time investment.

For couples on a quest to share the experience of culinary creation à deux, take note: Inside is a plethora of ideas on how to turn your kitchen time into quality time together. Whether playing DJ while your partner peels potatoes or chopping vegetables side by side, opportunities for maximizing efficiency and fun abound, taking the stress out of the cooking process and putting the pleasure back in.

Whether you're an experienced chef or a newbie in the kitchen, one thing remains a constant: Choosing to prepare a vegan meal is a wonderful way to integrate more healthy foods into your diet, lessen your environmental impact, and nourish yourself without doing harm to animals. Crack this book open and you'll discover tempting plant-based recipes that take the mystery out of cooking, with loads of tips for making the culinary process creative and fun.

CHAPTER 1

GETTING STARTED

Right now is an amazing time to be vegan. Not only is the lifestyle being embraced by millions of people worldwide as a solution to myriad global problems, but veganism also has the seal of approval of a growing coterie of celebrities who are helping propel the idea of plant-based eating into the mainstream, making it more acceptable and accessible. Today, the edible possibilities are practically limitless. More and more restaurants are adding vegan items to their menus, and grocery stores are filling their aisles with cruelty-free convenience foods that were once the exclusive domain of omnivores: (dairy-free) cheeses, (mock) meats, and (plant-based) milks, to name a few.

Why now? The reasons are plentiful and pretty straightforward. Animals are the clear winners when we choose a vegan diet, and many of us who are attracted to the idea of eating a plant-based diet are motivated by concern for animals and their welfare. Choosing to eliminate animal products is a way of walking our talk, and of taking a stand for something we believe in. Our health is another strong consideration for adopting a plant-based diet. The National Institutes of Health (NIH) recently released the results of a study indicating that people who consume plant-based diets live longer than their meat-and-dairy-eating counterparts. Yet another study, the results of which were published in the *Journal of the American Medical Association* (JAMA), indicate that vegans are at lower risk for hypertension.

You might have noticed that more and more card-carrying environmentalists are proudly flashing their vegan credentials when spreading the word about saving the planet, and with good reason: Animal agriculture—including dairy farming and egg production—is the main source of groundwater pollution in the United States, and a leading contributor to greenhouse gas emissions around the world. It's no longer a secret that the easiest step you can take to lighten your footprint on the planet is to adopt a low-impact vegan diet.

Whatever your reasons for taking the plant-based path (either some of the time or all of the time), you've got a lot to be excited about. Not only are you taking a kinder, healthier, and more environmentally sound route, but you're also choosing to celebrate the earth's bounty with every bite.

10 Tips on Happy Veganism

➤ **Go Easy on Yourself** Whether you're dabbling or diving head first into veganism, remember to go easy on yourself. Take your time to experiment with different ethnic cuisines, to familiarize yourself with tofu, tempeh, and TVP (textured vegetable protein). Discover the difference between almond and rice milk. Becoming an expert doesn't happen overnight. Lifestyle changes, big and small, have a learning curve, and it's important to learn to love the process and accept the little fumbles along the way to make the most of it.

➤ **Visit a Farm Sanctuary** Connecting with rescued farm animals is one of the most wonderfully life-enriching ways to cement your good intentions to partake in a lifestyle that causes the least harm. Meeting castoffs from the dairy industry or battery hens rescued from a life of egg production is guaranteed to make you feel all warm inside (because, let's face it, animals are cute), but will also put a face to some of the foods you no longer consume, which you won't be able to help but feel good about.

- ➤ **Join a Community Garden or CSA** If you've never tasted a carrot, beet, or potato freshly plucked from the soil, you'll be dazzled by the difference in flavor compared to the standard fare available in supermarkets. If you're not partial to the plant kingdom yet, you will be after joining your local community garden, where you'll meet new people while getting your hands dirty. Don't have one near you? Try joining a CSA (community supported agriculture) instead, and count on locally grown produce delivered to your door every week.

- ➤ **Mix It Up** You'll be astounded by how many cultures have plant-based cuisine at their cores. Make an effort to explore the native foods of far-flung countries, including Lebanon, Ethiopia, and Vietnam. Experiment in the kitchen by veganizing some of your more familiar go-tos, such as Mexican (try the Mexican Black Bean Salad on page 48) or Italian (our Creamy Artichoke Pizza recipe is on page 131). Shop at ethnic markets, try a new restaurant, or dig into this book's recipe vault for make-it-at-home ideas.

- ➤ **Meetup for Fun & Support** Don't know about Meetup? Get thee to the nearest computer, at once! Meetup is an online social media site connecting groups of people with shared interests, with the ultimate goal of meeting in person to enjoy activities en masse. Look for vegan cooking Meetups, potlucks, activist outings, and more. Check Meetup.com to see what's happening in your area. Can't find anything? Start your own group!

- ➤ **Browse the Blogosphere** If you find inspiration in cookbooks, you'll find even more good stuff in the never-ending blogosphere black hole. If you get your jollies just looking at photos and drooling, there's plenty of content out there to whet your whistle. If tried-and-true recipes are what you seek, rest assured that every trial, tribulation, and food-related success story has been chronicled online. Weeding through (and reading through) the possibilities to find something you resonate with is half the fun. For a great list of vegan websites, check out the Resources section on page 165.

- ➤ **Visit Your Doctor** Hundreds of thousands of people who've made the switch to a plant-based diet have experienced surprising health advantages, from lowered cholesterol levels to clearer skin and weight loss. Good health is something that should never be taken for granted, however, so it's always a good idea when making a lifestyle shift to pay a visit to your general practitioner or primary-care physician. He or she can advise you on what, if any, supplements you should be taking, and can do a blood panel to check your cholesterol levels and establish a baseline for later comparison.

HOW TO PARE FOR PAIRS

Sometimes eyeballing doesn't cut the mustard; what looks like just the right amount for a double portion in the measuring cup might translate to not enough lentils for your salad or too much marinara for your lasagna, which means wasted time and resources. Until you're a Level 1 Master Chef (which you will be after cooking your way through this book), measuring is mandatory! Commit these measurements to memory and you'll always have perfectly-portioned pasta, just-right rice, and lentils sans leftovers.

> **RICE**
> One cup of dried rice (and two cups of water) is just the right amount of rice for a two-person meal.

> **OATMEAL**
> One cup of dried oatmeal (and two cups of water) will make a hot, wholesome breakfast for two.

> **SPAGHETTI AND LINGUINI**
> Like most pasta, two ounces is the standard measurement for one person, but what if you don't have a scale? No problem! Grab a handful of noodles and measure the diameter using your thumb and index finger, which is about the size of a quarter. When cooking for two, double those quarters into fifty cents.

> **SMALL-SIZE PASTA**
> For macaroni, penne, and rigatoni noodles, two portions is equal to one cup of dried pasta, which will practically double in size once cooked.

> **BEANS**
> Cooked beans are most often found in 15- to 16-ounce cans, which just happens to be a perfect portion size for two people.

> **LENTILS**
> Like rice, you'll want a ratio of one cup dried lentils to two cups water to serve two hungry diners.

➤ **Prepare to Share** Let's just say that you made your first pumpkin pie, and it was so tasty that your girlfriend didn't even notice the difference between yours (made with coconut milk) and Grandma's (laden with eggs). And let's just say that you felt so confident about this here pie that you decided to prepare one to bring to the family Thanksgiving party, and that you decided not to tell anyone it was vegan, and they devoured every last slice. That "Yes!" feeling you got? It can be yours often and regularly if you cook vegan foods and share them with others. Try baking a batch of dark-chocolate chip cookies, or passing around a tray of Whoopee! Pies (page 143) at your next book club meeting to get that winning feeling.

➤ **Spring for a Splurge** Treat yourself to a meal at a gourmet vegan restaurant from time to time, to remind yourself just how amazing and creative a vegan diet can be with seasonal menus. In Los Angeles, head to the celebrity haunt Crossroads and tuck into Truffled Leek Flatbread; in New York City, try the legendary Candle 79's unforgettable Seitan Piccata; in Philadelphia, you've got to book a table at the hottest spot in town, Vedge, where Lemon Drop Melon Carpaccio with Roasted Red Pepper and Canary Melon Sorbet await you.

➤ **Read All About It** Vegan books now have their own section at the bookstore—and we're not just talking about cookbooks. Seek and you shall find magazines, lifestyle guides, and tomes dedicated to plant-based nutrition that'll get you pumped to make compassionate, healthy food choices every day. For a list of reading material to get you started, see our Resources on page 165.

Divide and Conquer

If, as the old saying goes, "two heads are better than one," then four hands are surely better than two. Apply that doubled-up logic to cooking duty, and mealtimes are transformed into opportunities for togetherness with tasty results. These tips will fuel you with ideas for sharing the fun before breaking bread.

Chef and Prep Cook

Maybe in your home, there's one clear "boss." If that person happens to be you, then it's your job to direct your prep cook like a pro would. Have your kitchen sidekick peel your garlic cloves, chop onions, and rinse the rice, so you can concentrate on following recipes without interrupting the culinary flow.

Mise en Place

This fancy French term translates literally into "put into place." If you've watched even one cooking show in your entire life, you'll have noticed that the chefs always have their spices, liquids, and dry goods all measured out and ready to toss into the pot—and that's what your mise en place person will do while you make the magic.

Clean Team

It's the easiest division of labor imaginable in the kitchen; one of you cooks while the other one cleans up. Tip: The dishwashing job is made simpler when you clean as you go, so you're not left with a daunting pile of dirty plates at the end of the night.

Time Management

If you've ever overcooked the linguini or burned a batch of cookies, that's probably because you didn't have your Time Manager on hand to help. A Time Manager's job is to make sure the pasta is al dente (while you concentrate on making the sauce), and the Garlicky Kale Crostini (page 62) perfectly golden without a hint of charring.

Shop-n-Chop

One of you does the shopping while the other does the cooking. Sounds simple, right? That's because it is! Spend 15 minutes meal-planning together before the week begins, then assign shopping and cooking duties. Trade off each week to keep it interesting.

Compost Kings and Queens

Hate grating carrots but don't mind a walk in the after-dinner dark to the compost pile or bin? The one peeling the potatoes gets to call it a night after the dining is done, while the Compost Queen (or King) is obliged to make her or his way into the great outdoors.

Music and Menu Pairings

Sometimes, it's the little touches that can bring magic to an everyday occasion. Take music, for example. Have your partner create a playlist to match the menu's tone, and see how much more enjoyable the dining experience can be. Try a little Dean Martin (That's Amore) with your Pasta Bolognese with Lentils (page 117) or a Bollywood soundtrack with your Curried Cauliflower Soup (page 82)

Maitre d' and Master Chef

Food prep is thirst-activating work, and there's nothing quite as helpful as having an attentive maitre d' to ensure that your libation is refreshed while you get crafty in the kitchen. While one of you cooks, the other can pour the lemonade, hot tea, or sparkling wine to ensure optimal cooking results.

10 Ingredients to Have on Hand

A well-stocked pantry is the foundation that will ensure every meal you sit down to enjoy is loaded with flavor and nutrients. With these staples at the ready, you'll be able to whip up hearty soups, filling pastas, savory rice dishes, and even desserts with just a few simple additions.

- **EVOO (Extra-Virgin Olive Oil)** This oil is loaded with monounsaturated fatty acids, making it one of the healthiest oils to incorporate into your diet. It's ideal for salad dressings and recipes that call for oil (including desserts), and can even be drizzled over toast in place of butter. Invest in a good-quality oil to add extra flavor to your recipes, and store in a cool, dark place to keep it fresher longer.

- **Canned Coconut Milk** Coconut milk adds an instant taste of luxury to anything. Whether making coconut cream to top your favorite pie or cup of cocoa, or pouring it into your curried vegetables, you can expect rich, creamy results.

- **Brown or White Rice** Rice is one of those pantry staples that, like pasta, offers sustenance, nourishment, and the perfect foundation for whatever flavorful extras you've got on hand. You can't go wrong topping it with sauce, using it as a base for grain salads, pairing it with beans for a burrito stuffing, or frying it up with some greens for a fast, savory meal.

- **Soy Sauce or Wheat-Free Tamari** Salt is good, but with soy sauce and tamari, you get an extra dimension of flavor that falls into the savory umami, or "fifth-flavor" spectrum, which also includes mushrooms, olives, and balsamic vinegar. We often think of soy sauce as a seasoning for Asian food, but it can also be used to add depth of flavor to pasta sauces and bean-based dishes.

- **Tomato Paste in a Tube** The person who invented tomato paste in a tube deserves an award. Squeeze out just what you need for that night's Amazing Minestrone (page 85) or Essential Marinara (page 150), and then stick it back in the fridge without the added step of storing leftovers in a glass jar or fumbling with the aluminum foil.

- ➤ **Canned Beans** Beans are a vegan cook's best friend. They add protein and flavor to any recipe, and a good dose of healthy fats. Puréed, they make a rich dip; roasted, they make a tasty snack. Try tossing some in your next pasta sauce, soup, or salad to add heft and flavor.

- ➤ **Onions and Garlic** These two are stars in the culinary galaxy, and staples in the cuisines of many cultures. Store in a cool, dry place, and reach for one or both to bring out the flavors of other ingredients in soups, stews, and sauces.

- ➤ **Rice Noodles** The magic of rice noodles is their lickety-split prep time. Just soak in hot water for three minutes and voilà! You've got the start of a delectable meal. Add them to your favorite broth for a slurpy noodle soup, or toss them in a pan with vegetables and a dash of curry powder for a one-pot meal.

- ➤ **Textured Vegetable Protein/Soy Curls** For those times when you just want to nosh something that you can really sink your teeth into. For both texture and versatility, reach for textured vegetable protein—often sold as Soy Curls. Soak them in water, then simmer with your favorite seasoning, and use in place of meat in traditional recipes.

- ➤ **Cashews and Almonds** The high fat content in nuts makes them so alluring, and it's also what makes them so versatile. They're great sources of instant energy when munched as a snack or tossed onto salads, but they can also be transformed into amazing milks and cheeses (like our Cashew Crème on page 153).

MONEY-SAVING TIPS

A plant-based diet is so much more than just healthy and delicious; it's economical, too—especially if you prepare your meals using fewer packaged products and more whole foods. Whittle the portions down to two servings and you've just stretched your pennies even further—without feeling the pinch. These easy-to-implement ideas will save you money and add value to your culinary experiences.

➤ **BUY NON-PERISHABLES IN BULK.**
If you've got the storage space in your pantry, go ahead and buy the jumbo sack of rice, the extra-large bag of peppercorns, and other non-perishable items that come in gargantuan sizes. Buying in bulk is generally more affordable—as long as you eventually end up eating everything.

➤ **INVEST IN SMALL-SIZE COOKWARE.**
Spending a bit of money on cookware tailored for two portions will pay off in the long run by eliminating waste and facilitating efficiency. In a pinch, bread loaf pans can replace a standard casserole dish, and pie pans can double as cookie sheets.

➤ **GO NATURAL.**
Shopping for fresh produce at traditional grocery stores means buying entire bunches of carrots, heads of lettuce, and bags of potatoes. Instead, look to natural-food stores and farmers' markets where you can bag your own baby greens, beets, and other fresh produce in tailor-made sizes.

➤ **FREEZE THE FLAVOR.**
Fresh herbs are one of the few edibles hard to find in diminutive sizes. To preserve the fresh flavor of your Italian parsley, dill, or other herbs, toss them in the blender or food processor with water and freeze in ice-cube trays for later use.

➤ **THINK SMALL.**
When shopping for non-dairy milks, look for the smallest sizes available (usually 8 ounces) to eliminate waste. Coconut milk is also sold in diminutive 5.5-ounce cans that are perfect for two-person portions of Thai curry and Tom Kha soup.

BRILLIANT BREAKFASTS

PREP TIME:
10 MINUTES

COOK TIME:
20 MINUTES

Loaded Baked Potato Scones

Toast is a perfectly acceptable breakfast option, but it doesn't have quite the same Sunday morning appeal as a savory breakfast scone. This recipe mimics the flavor of a baked potato topped with all your favorites, and would taste just as delightful served alongside your breakfast scramble as it would a warming bowl of chili.

1. Preheat the oven to 400°F.

2. In a medium bowl, combine the flour, baking powder, and salt.

3. Add the margarine and combine to reach a crumbly consistency, then add the cheese and stir to combine.

4. In a small bowl, combine the potato, soy milk, and scallions.

5. Add to the flour mixture.

6. On a lightly-floured cutting board, knead the dough until pliable.

7. Shape into a small circle, then slice into four triangles and bake on a lightly oiled baking sheet for 20 minutes. Serve warm.

¾ cup all-purpose flour
1 teaspoon baking powder
½ teaspoon salt
2 tablespoons vegan margarine
¼ cup grated vegan cheese (such as Daiya)
1 small potato, peeled, steamed, and mashed
2 tablespoons soy milk
2 scallions, thinly sliced

Black Currant Scones with Cashew Crème

The sweetness of currants gets a little zing from lemon zest in these traditional gems. Cashew crème makes an excellent stand-in for the clotted cream that these might be served with during a traditional English tea. If currants aren't your favorite, try substituting either brown or golden raisins, dried cranberries, or, if you're in the mood for an indulgence, vegan chocolate chips!

PREP TIME:
10 MINUTES

COOK TIME:
20 MINUTES

¾ cup all-purpose flour
1 teaspoon baking powder
½ teaspoon salt
2 tablespoons sugar
Pinch ground cinnamon
2 tablespoons vegan
    margarine
2 tablespoons non-dairy milk
2 tablespoons dried currants
Zest of 1 lemon
2 tablespoons Cashew Crème
    (page 153), blended with
    1 tablespoon maple syrup

1. Preheat the oven to 400°F.

2. In a medium bowl, combine the flour, baking powder, salt, sugar, and cinnamon.

3. Add the margarine and non-dairy milk. Combine until you get a crumbly dough.

4. On a lightly-floured cutting board, knead the dough until pliable, working in the currants and lemon zest a little at a time.

5. Shape the dough into a small circle.

6. Slice into four triangles and bake on a lightly oiled baking sheet for 20 minutes.

7. Serve warm with a dollop of Cashew Crème.

PREP TIME:
10 MINUTES

Overnight Oats à la Elvis

You don't need to be a fan of The King (or even know who he is!) to appreciate these overnight oats, which taste a lot like Elvis's beloved peanut butter and banana sandwich. In this wholesome morning meal in a bowl, you do the prep work the evening before. All you have to do in the morning is roll out of bed and head to the table.

1. In a small bowl, mash the bananas and peanut butter to combine.

2. Add the cinnamon, vanilla, oats, and milk and stir to combine.

3. Divide the banana-peanut butter-oat mixture into two bowls.

4. Top each bowl with 1 tablespoon of maple syrup.

5. Cover and let sit overnight or for a minimum of 4 hours before serving.

1 ripe banana, mashed
¼ cup peanut butter
½ teaspoon ground cinnamon
½ teaspoon vanilla extract
1 cup rolled oats
1 cup non-dairy milk
2 tablespoons maple syrup or agave nectar, divided

Tropical Chia Breakfast Bowl

GLUTEN-FREE
QUICK & EASY

PREP TIME:
10 MINUTES

Chia seeds are the new darlings of the breakfast world. Why? Because they're easy to prepare, a good source of fiber and omega-3 fatty acids, and they're adaptable to a variety of different culinary interpretations. This recipe relies on a combination of fresh and dried fruit to give it flavor and texture.

2 cups non-dairy milk

½ cup chia seeds

2 tablespoons shredded, dried coconut

Pinch salt

½ teaspoon vanilla extract

2 tablespoons maple syrup or agave nectar

1 small banana, thinly sliced

1. In a medium-size bowl, combine the non-dairy milk, chia seeds, coconut, salt, vanilla, and maple syrup.

2. Refrigerate overnight (or a minimum of 1 hour).

3. To serve, stir the chia mixture, then divide into two bowls.

4. Top each bowl with sliced banana and extra non-dairy milk if desired.

TIP: *To take this pudding to decadent heights, replace half the amount of non-dairy milk with coconut milk. One small (5.5-ounce) can equals roughly one cup.*

PREP TIME:
10 MINUTES

Glorious Green Smoothie

There's a good reason for the popularity of green smoothies: They taste great! They're also filling, and, when prepared with the right ingredients, incredibly nutritious. This recipe calls on spinach to give it its namesake color, and a secret green ingredient—avocado—to give it its creaminess and a healthy dose of good fats.

1. In a blender, combine all the ingredients and purée until smooth. If the smoothie is too thick, add a bit of water to thin.

2. To serve, pour into two glasses.

TIP: *Anyone who owns one will tell you a high-speed blender is worth the investment. Besides giving smoothies their trademark creamy consistency, a high-speed blender is also ideal for puréeing soups and making nut cheeses.*

2 cups baby spinach leaves, packed

1 small, ripe avocado, halved, scooped, and chopped

1 ripe pear, cored and chopped

1 tablespoon maple syrup or agave nectar

1 cup rice milk

1 teaspoon vanilla extract

Chocolate Power Smoothie

In some parts of the world, chocolate is consumed for breakfast, and why not?! It's full of antioxidants and trace minerals that support your health. This smoothie tastes like dessert and will sate you straight through to lunchtime.

1 large banana, sliced

3 Medjool dates, pitted (or five regular dates, pitted)

2 tablespoons almond butter

3 tablespoons raw cacao powder

1 teaspoon flaxseed, finely ground

2 cups non-dairy milk

½ teaspoon vanilla extract

Pinch salt

Add all the ingredients and blend in a high-speed blender until smooth and creamy.

TIP: *There are an astounding number of date varieties available, but the most common varieties sold in the United States are the Deglet Noor and Medjool dates. The latter are a decadent treat, with a price to match. Sticky, chewy, and slightly larger than standard dates, they're worth the splurge, though for this recipe, either variety will work.*

Crunchy Cardamom Quinoa Porridge

If you're not well acquainted with quinoa yet, the time to get to know each other is now. This quick-cooking grain is a great substitute for rice when making savory dishes, and in this hot breakfast cereal, it stands in for oatmeal. The crunch in this recipe comes from toasted almonds, which can be prepared in minutes with the help of a toaster oven or hot skillet.

1. Combine the quinoa, non-dairy milk, vanilla, cardamom, and salt.

2. Cover and cook over low heat, stirring occasionally, for 20 minutes, or until the quinoa expands and turns tender.

3. To serve, ladle into two bowls.

4. Top with the maple syrup, chopped nuts, and nectarine (if using).

1 cup quinoa

2 cups non-dairy milk

½ teaspoon vanilla

⅛ teaspoon ground cardamom powder

Pinch salt

2 tablespoons maple syrup or agave nectar

¼ cup toasted almonds, roughly chopped

1 ripe nectarine or peach, chopped (optional)

Texas Two-Step Tofu Scramble

GLUTEN-FREE
QUICK & EASY
NUT-FREE

This summertime scramble gets its Southern-style flavor from a combination of fresh corn kernels and sun-ripened bell pepper. For more spice, give each serving a splash of Tabasco sauce or another hot sauce of your choosing.

PREP TIME:
10 MINUTES

COOK TIME:
15 MINUTES

1 (8-ounce) package of extra-firm tofu, drained and patted dry

Salt

Freshly ground black pepper

1 teaspoon chili powder or smoked paprika

1 teaspoon extra-virgin olive oil

1 small onion, roughly chopped

1 garlic clove, finely chopped

1 small red bell pepper, roughly chopped

Corn kernels, freshly scraped from ear of corn (about ½ cup)

1 small jalapeño pepper, minced

Fresh cilantro, for garnish

1. In a large bowl, crumble the tofu and season with salt, pepper, and chili powder.

2. Add the oil to a nonstick skillet.

3. Sauté the onion over medium heat, stirring, for 2 minutes.

4. Add the garlic and cook for one minute more.

5. Add the tofu, red bell pepper, and corn.

6. Sauté, stirring, for 10 minutes.

7. Stir in the jalapeño, stir, and remove from the heat.

8. To serve, spoon onto plates and garnish with the fresh cilantro.

TIP: *To give your tofu even more of a toothsome chew, stick the entire unopened package in the freezer for a minimum of 24 hours. The night before you prepare your scramble, pull out the package and allow it to thaw on a countertop overnight. In the morning, proceed as you would with regular tofu.*

PREP TIME:
10 MINUTES

COOK TIME:
20 MINUTES

Green Chile Chilaquiles

Chilaquiles is a traditional Mexican breakfast dish that's filling without being overly spicy. This version is made with tofu and mild green chiles, but you can add fire to your rendition with a dash of bright-green Habanero sauce in a bottle.

1. In a large nonstick skillet, heat the oil over medium heat. Add the tortilla slices and onion.

2. Sauté, stirring, for 5 minutes.

3. Add the tofu and green chiles. Season with salt.

4. Sauté for 10 minutes more, adding water if necessary to keep the chilaquiles soft and pliable.

5. Remove the chilaquiles from the heat and sprinkle with the grated cheese (if using).

6. To serve, squeeze with lime and sprinkle with cilantro.

TIP: *If your weekly menu plan includes a few Mexican-inspired dishes, you'll want to have fresh cilantro handy to add authentic flavor. To keep cilantro fresh and flavorful for a week or more, place the cilantro bouquet stems-down in a glass of water, cover with a plastic bag, and secure with a rubber band. Store in the refrigerator and use as needed.*

1 tablespoon **extra-virgin olive oil**

2 **corn tortillas,** sliced into thin strips

1 small **onion,** finely diced

1 (8-ounce) package **extra-firm tofu,** drained, patted dry, and crumbled

1 (4-ounce) can chopped **green chiles**

Salt

2 tablespoons **water**

¼ cup grated **vegan jack-style cheese,** such as Daiya (optional)

Squeeze of **lime,** for garnish

Fresh **cilantro,** for garnish

Sweet & Savory Potato-Kale Hash

GLUTEN-FREE
QUICK & EASY
NUT-FREE

Warming and nourishing, this simple hash is easy to prepare and full of flavor. If you don't have access to kale, use chopped chard, or even spinach. Yams would work in place of sweet potatoes, or even standard-issue spuds would do the trick.

PREP TIME:
10 MINUTES

COOK TIME:
20 MINUTES

Extra-virgin olive oil,
for sautéing
1 small onion, finely chopped
1 teaspoon ground cumin
1 garlic clove, minced
1 large sweet potato, peeled
and cut into small dice
(about 2 cups)
1 cup finely chopped kale
½ cup water
Juice of 1 lemon (optional)
Salt
Freshly ground black pepper

1. In a large nonstick skillet over medium-high heat, add the oil, onion, and cumin. Sauté, stirring for two minutes.

2. Add the garlic, sweet potatoes, and kale. Sauté for two minutes more, or until the garlic is fragrant.

3. Add the water. Steam, covered, for five minutes, stirring once or twice, until the potatoes and kale are tender.

4. To serve, squeeze the lemon (if using) over the hash. Season with salt and paper.

TIP: *The squeeze of lemon in this dish is optional, but the acid in the citrus will help your body absorb more of the iron available in the kale, chard, or spinach.*

PREP TIME:
10 MINUTES

COOK TIME:
20 MINUTES

Pile-It-On Potatoes

Potatoes are the ultimate comfort food, and this brunch-worthy recipe pairs the humble spud with a bouquet of flavorful add-ons for one very hearty morning meal. The foundation is simple and tasty all on its own, but it's worth going all out and piling on the extras.

1. Preheat the oven to 450°F.

2. In a medium bowl, add the potatoes, olive oil, and onion. Season with salt.

3. Spread the potato-onion mixture on a cookie sheet and roast for 20 minutes, turning once or twice.

4. To serve, remove the potatoes from the oven and divide between two plates.

5. Top with the tomato, avocado, tempeh bacon, a dollop of Cashew Crème, and scallion, then sprinkle with pepper.

2 medium russet potatoes, peeled, rinsed, and chopped into small dice

1 tablespoon extra-virgin olive oil

1 onion, peeled and chopped into small dice

Salt

1 tomato, chopped

1 avocado, halved, scooped, and chopped

2 slices tempeh or other vegan bacon, crumbled

2 tablespoons Cashew Crème (page 153)

1 scallion, thinly sliced

Freshly ground black pepper

Chickpea-and-Greens Crêpe

This savory crêpe is simple yet flavorful, and tastes as good cold as it does warm. The batter improves with time, so making it the night before and storing in the refrigerator is a perfectly good idea that'll save you time in the morning.

PREP TIME:
10 MINUTES

COOK TIME:
30 MINUTES

½ cup chickpea flour

1 cup water

1 teaspoon extra-virgin olive oil

¼ teaspoon cumin powder

½ teaspoon salt

1 cup chopped spinach, packed

1 scallion, thinly sliced

Freshly ground black pepper (optional)

1. Preheat the oven to 450°F.

2. In a medium bowl, combine the flour, water, oil, cumin, and salt. Stir to combine, and let the batter rest for a minimum of 1 hour to allow the flavors to marry.

3. Add the chopped spinach and scallion. Stir to combine.

4. Pour the batter into an oiled pie pan. Bake for 30 minutes, or until the crêpe is golden brown. To serve, dust with pepper (if using).

TIP: *Chickpea flour—also known as besan flour—is a staple in Indian cuisine. So, if you've got a South Asian grocery store in your neighborhood, this is a great place to source this recipe's main ingredient.*

PREP TIME:
10 MINUTES

COOK TIME:
15 MINUTES

Crêpes with Lemony Cashew Crème

Crêpes are often reserved for special occasions, but considering how easy they are to prepare and how delightful they taste, they really ought to be an everyday affair. These are filled with a creamy citrus sauce, and are at once filling and refreshing. Wash them down with a small cup of espresso to give your breakfast extra French flavor.

1. In a large bowl, combine the flour, baking powder, salt, and milk. Whisk together until smooth. The batter should be thin.

2. In a small bowl, blend the Cashew Crème, maple syrup, lemon juice and zest.

3. In a large nonstick skillet over medium-high heat, add a small knob of coconut oil, swirling to coat the pan. Ladle in ¼ of the batter mixture, and cook for 1 to 2 minutes on each side. Continue with the remaining batter.

4. To serve, spoon a tablespoon of crème inside each crêpe, spread to cover, and gently fold into a cylindrical shape. Garnish with powdered sugar (if using).

TIP: *Pesticide residue gets lodged in the skin of conventional citrus fruit, which are often treated with a wax coating, too. When following a recipe that calls for lemon zest, always choose organic to avoid ingesting funky waxes and pesticides.*

¾ cup all-purpose flour
1 teaspoon baking powder
Pinch salt
¾ cup non-dairy milk
¼ cup Cashew Crème
 (page 153)
1 tablespoon maple syrup or
 agave nectar
Juice and zest of 1 lemon
Coconut oil, for frying
Powdered sugar, to garnish
 (optional)

Praline Pancakes

Praline is just a fancy term for nuts that have been toasted with a bit of sugar—or, in this case, maple syrup. If you don't have access to pecans, you can substitute walnuts or even whole hazelnuts.

PREP TIME:
10 MINUTES

COOK TIME:
20 MINUTES

¾ cup all-purpose flour
1 teaspoon baking powder
Pinch salt
½ cup non-dairy milk
½ teaspoon vanilla extract
½ cup walnut or pecan halves
¼ teaspoon ground cinnamon
2 tablespoons maple syrup
Coconut oil, for frying
Additional maple syrup,
    to taste

1. Preheat the oven to 400°F.

2. In a large bowl, combine the flour, baking powder, salt, milk, and vanilla. Whisk until smooth.

3. In a small bowl, combine the walnuts, cinnamon, and maple syrup. Spread on a baking sheet and toast in the oven for 3 to 5 minutes, checking after the third minute to prevent burning. Remove from the oven and allow to cool while you prepare the pancakes.

4. In a large nonstick skillet, add a knob of coconut oil and ladle in two pancakes-worth of batter. Cook for 2 minutes on each side. Continue the process with the remaining batter.

5. To serve, divide the pancakes into two servings and top with maple syrup and pralines.

TIP: *Nuts will stay fresh for several months if stored in a tightly sealed container in the freezer.*

Classic French Toast

This recipe will take you back to special childhood breakfasts of yore. This version replaces the standard egg-based batter with an improved version made with banana and cornstarch. For best results, drench with maple syrup before serving, or, if you're feeling extra festive, top with a generous dusting of powdered sugar.

1. In a blender, combine the banana, cornstarch, milk, salt, and cinnamon. Purée until smooth.

2. Arrange the bread slices in a casserole dish and cover with the banana-cornstarch mixture, turning once to coat both sides. Let the bread soak up the mixture for 5 minutes.

3. In a nonstick skillet over medium-high heat, add the oil, followed by four of the bread slices.

4. Cook for 3 to 4 minutes on each side, or until golden. Repeat with the second batch of bread slices.

5. Serve with maple syrup or a dusting of powdered sugar.

1 small banana, sliced
2 teaspoons cornstarch
¾ cup non-dairy milk
Pinch salt
¼ teaspoon ground cinnamon
4 slices of your favorite bread, sliced in half on the diagonal
2 teaspoons coconut oil, divided, for frying
Maple syrup, for serving
Powdered sugar, for serving

Easy Cheesy Grits

QUICK & EASY
NUT-FREE

PREP TIME:
10 MINUTES

COOK TIME:
20 MINUTES

If you grew up anywhere near the South, you know the comfort-in-a-bowl that grits supply. Every good Southern cook has his or her own take on this timeless recipe, and ditching dairy does not mean sacrificing this homey staple. This version is great on its own, and also serves as a stellar base for garlicky greens or tempeh bacon.

1¼ cups water
Pinch salt
½ cup grits
1 teaspoon vegan margarine
¼ cup grated vegan cheese, such as Daiya
Freshly ground black pepper

1. In a small saucepan, combine the water and salt. Bring to a boil.

2. Slowly pour in the grits, stirring constantly.

3. Add the margarine and lower the heat to simmer. Cook for 5 minutes, stirring regularly.

4. When the grits have reached an oatmeal-like consistency, remove from the heat and stir in the grated cheese.

5. Ladle into bowls, and serve immediately with pepper.

Curried Mushroom-Tempeh Scramble

Tempeh is a whole-food, cultured soy "meat" that's full of protein and easy to digest. Like tofu, it has a bland, unassuming flavor that adapts well to different kinds of seasonings. Here, tempeh is paired with mushrooms and a fragrant curry powder for a memorable morning meal.

1. In a medium nonstick skillet over medium-high heat, add the oil and onion. Sauté for 2 minutes, or until onion the becomes fragrant. Add the curry powder and stir.

2. Add the mushrooms and tempeh.

3. Cook, stirring, for 5 minutes, or until the mushrooms shrink to half their size.

4. Add the kale, soy sauce, and water. Stir to combine, lower the heat, and cover. In 5 to 7 minutes, when the water has evaporated and the greens are soft, the scramble is ready to serve.

TIP: *If you happen to notice a few little black spots on your tempeh, don't worry! That's a naturally occurring mold that is harmless and perfectly edible.*

1 teaspoon extra-virgin olive oil

1 small onion, finely chopped

1 teaspoon curry powder

5 cremini or other firm mushrooms, thinly sliced

1 (8-ounce) package plain tempeh, chopped into small dice

¼ cup finely chopped kale, chard, or other green

1 teaspoon soy sauce

2 tablespoons water

Warming Asian Vegetable Porridge

QUICK & EASY
NUT-FREE

PREP TIME:
10 MINUTES

COOK TIME:
5 MINUTES

If you savored bowls of Cream of Wheat as a kid, you'll probably like this savory grown-up version made with rice (sometimes called "rice farina" or "creamy rice") instead of wheat. The consistency is the same, but the flavor profile is skewed toward the savory instead of the sweet. The toasted sesame oil is the key flavor element.

2 cups water
½ teaspoon salt
½ cup Cream of Rice cereal
1 small turnip, cut into cubes and steamed
1 scallion, thinly sliced
Soy sauce or tamari
Toasted sesame oil

1. In a medium saucepan over medium-high heat, bring the water and salt to a boil.

2. Slowly pour in the cereal, stirring with a whisk until well blended.

3. Reduce the heat to low and simmer, stirring constantly, for 1 minute, then remove from the heat.

4. To serve, ladle the porridge into bowls. Top each with half of the turnip, half of the scallions, and a generous drizzle of soy sauce and sesame oil.

PREP TIME:
10 MINUTES

COOK TIME:
30 MINUTES

Nutty Olive Oil Granola

Like everything else made from scratch, homemade granola tastes so much better than anything you could find in the store. This recipe calls for a combination of seeds and dried fruit, but you could easily swap out the seeds for nuts, or add another dried fruit of your choosing.

1. Preheat the oven to 350°F.

2. In a large bowl, combine the oats, pumpkin seeds, sesame seeds, coconut flakes, maple syrup, oil, cinnamon, and salt.

3. On a parchment-lined baking sheet, spread the granola mixture and toast for 30 minutes, turning twice, until golden brown.

4. Remove the granola from the oven and allow it to cool.

5. Add the apricots and stir to combine.

6. To serve, divide the granola into two bowls and douse in your favorite non-dairy milk.

1 cup rolled oats

¼ cup raw pumpkin seeds, hulled

2 tablespoons raw sesame seeds

2 tablespoons dried coconut flakes

2 tablespoons maple syrup

2 tablespoons extra-virgin olive oil

½ teaspoon ground cinnamon

Pinch salt

¼ cup finely chopped dried apricots or dates

Non-dairy milk, for serving

Cornmeal Griddle Cakes

This old-fashioned recipe tastes like something you'd find on the menu in a Southern diner. Serve with a side of tempeh bacon, or a fresh fruit salad, and don't skimp on the maple syrup or jam! More is better with this recipe.

PREP TIME:
10 MINUTES

COOK TIME:
12 MINUTES

½ teaspoon salt

¾ cup water

¾ cup fine cornmeal

1 tablespoon extra-virgin olive oil, plus extra for frying

½ cup seasonal berries (strawberries, blackberries, blueberries)

Jam or maple syrup, for serving

1. In a medium saucepan over high heat, bring the salt and water to a boil. Gradually pour in the cornmeal, whisking constantly until fully combined.

2. Remove from the heat and stir in the oil, followed by the berries. The consistency should be liquid enough to pour. Add more water if needed to thin.

3. In a large nonstick skillet over medium-high heat, pour a bit of oil, then ladle in ¼ cup of batter for each cake. Cook for 3 minutes on each side, or until golden.

4. To serve, top with your favorite jam or maple syrup.

PREP TIME:
10 MINUTES

COOK TIME:
15 MINUTES

Avocado Benedict

There's no need to wait for a special occasion to prepare a breakfast with "Benedict" in the title. This savory morning treat takes less than 30 minutes to prepare, and is full of healthy fats and protein.

To make the Hollandaise sauce

1. In a small saucepan over medium-high heat, add the cornstarch-water mixture, lemon juice, nutritional yeast, salt, and saffron (if using).

2. Bring to a boil, stirring constantly.

3. Reduce the heat and simmer, stirring, for 3 minutes, or until thick and bubbly.

4. Remove from the heat. Set the sauce aside.

To make the Benedict base

1. Toast the English muffins until golden brown, and rub each slice with half of a garlic clove.

2. Top each muffin half with two slices of tempeh bacon and half of the avocado slices.

3. Spoon the Hollandaise sauce over each avocado-topped muffin.

4. Garnish with pepper and paprika.

5. Serve immediately.

For the Hollandaise sauce

1 teaspoon cornstarch dissolved in 1 cup cold water or soy milk

Juice of 1 lemon

¼ cup nutritional yeast flakes

½ teaspoon salt

Pinch saffron or turmeric for color (optional)

Freshly ground black pepper

For the Benedict base

1 English muffin, split in half

1 garlic clove, halved

4 slices prepared tempeh bacon or other vegan bacon

1 small avocado, halved, pitted, and cut into thin slices

Freshly ground black pepper

Smoked paprika

Fruit & Oatmeal

Warming, nourishing, and unbelievably filling thanks to a healthy dose of fiber
from the oats, this simple breakfast is worth repeating several mornings a week.
In winter, when fresh fruit is less accessible, substitute dried fruit, such as
raisins, chopped dates, or figs for sweetness and texture.

COOK TIME:
10 MINUTES

1 cup whole oats

2 cups water

pinch of salt

1 teaspoon cinnamon

Non-dairy yogurt, to taste
(optional)

Maple syrup, to taste
(optional)

½ cup seasonal berries
(blueberries, strawberries,
raspberries) or sliced
fresh fruit

1 tablespoon sunflower seeds

1. Combine the oats, water, and pinch of salt. Cover and cook over
medium heat, stirring occasionally, for 10 minutes, or until the oats
are soft and most of the water has evaporated.

2. To serve, ladle oatmeal into bowls, sprinkle with cinnamon, then
top with yogurt, maple syrup, and fresh berries, then sprinkle with
sunflower seeds.

SATISFYING SALADS

Hearty Farro Salad

Farro is an ancient grain related to wheat. It has a toothsome bite and nutty flavor that marries well with the umami flavor of the mushrooms and crisp green beans in this salad. Enjoy this dish as meal in itself—it works equally well served either warm or cool.

1. In a saucepan over medium-high heat, combine farro and water. Simmer for 30 minutes, or until tender, draining any remaining liquid, if necessary.

2. While the farro cooks, heat the olive oil in a sauté pan over medium heat. Add the tofu and cook, stirring, until browned on all sides, about 10 minutes.

3. Remove the tofu from the pan and set aside. Add the mushrooms to the pan, and cook for 5 minutes, until lightly browned.

4. Add cooked farro, tofu, mushrooms, and green beans back to the pan, toss together, and cook for two minutes until warmed through.

TIP: *There are many pre-packaged marinated tofu options available these days, which means that customizing this recipe to your particular tastes is easier than ever. Teriyaki or sesame ginger flavors would work particularly well here.*

½ cup farro
1½ cups water
1 tablespoon olive oil
½ (8-ounce) package marinated tofu, cubed
½ cup sliced shiitake mushrooms
1 cup cooked green beans

Moroccan Eggplant Salad

North African cuisine makes good use of warming spices such as cinnamon and cumin, both of which make an appearance in this succulent salad. Serve with small cups of hot mint tea for an authentic taste of Morocco.

PREP TIME:
10 MINUTES

COOK TIME:
30 MINUTES

1 medium eggplant, cut into thick slices

2 tablespoons extra-virgin olive oil, divided

Salt

1 (15-ounce) can of chickpeas, drained and rinsed

1 large tomato, roughly chopped

1 small red onion, finely chopped

¼ cup roughly chopped cilantro

1 teaspoon dried cumin powder

⅛ teaspoon ground cinnamon

1 teaspoon agave nectar

Juice of 1 lemon

1. Preheat the oven to 475°F.

2. Arrange the eggplant slices on a baking sheet. Drizzle with 1 tablespoon oil, turning to coat both sides. Season with salt and bake in the oven for 30 minutes, turning once or twice, until tender and golden. When cool, chop the eggplant into thick chunks.

3. In a large bowl, add the eggplant, chickpeas, tomato, onion, and cilantro.

4. In a small bowl, add the cumin, cinnamon, agave nectar, lemon juice, remaining 1 tablespoon oil, and salt to taste. Whisk to combine, then pour over the chickpea-eggplant mixture.

5. Stir to combine.

6. Serve and enjoy.

TIP: *Toasting spices can bring out even more of their flavor, and that is especially true with cumin. In a nonstick skillet over medium heat, toast the powder for 30 to 40 seconds, shaking the pan to prevent burning, until fragrant.*

PREP TIME:
10 MINUTES

COOK TIME:
10 MINUTES

Mediterranean Artichoke Salad

This hearty salad carries the flavor of coastal Italy in every bite. To lighten up the flavors even more, you could serve this on a bed of arugula, romaine, or baby spinach leaves. Don't have artichoke hearts on hand? Substituting four or five roughly chopped oil-packed sun-dried tomatoes would give the same tangy flavor.

1. In a medium saucepan over high heat, bring the water to a boil. Add the pasta and cook for 5 to 7 minutes, or until al dente. Strain and rinse under cold water to halt the cooking process.

2. In a large bowl, combine the pasta, black olives, beans, and artichoke hearts. Stir to combine.

3. In a small bowl, add the garlic, vinegar, oil, oregano, and salt and pepper to taste. Whisk together until combined, then pour over the salad-pasta mixture and serve.

2 cups water

1 cup bowtie or other pasta

¼ cup roughly chopped pitted black olives, rinsed

1 (15-ounce) can cannellini beans or kidney beans, rinsed and drained

1 (14-ounce) can artichoke hearts, drained and roughly chopped

1 small garlic clove, minced

1 tablespoon red wine vinegar

1 tablespoon extra-virgin olive oil

½ teaspoon dried oregano

Salt

Freshly ground black pepper

Quinoa and Smoked Tofu Salad

Quinoa is at once light and filling. Here, it is combined with the savory flavor of smoked tofu and the freshness of juicy vegetables to create a complex orchestra of flavors. It tastes even better when the flavors have been allowed to mingle, so if you can handle it, wait an hour before serving.

PREP TIME:
10 MINUTES

COOK TIME:
25 MINUTES

2 cups water

1 cup quinoa

1 tablespoon extra-virgin olive oil

Juice of 1 lemon

1 small garlic clove, minced

1 (8-ounce) package smoked tofu, cut into small dice

½ cucumber, peeled, seeded, and diced

1 small red bell pepper, seeded and diced

1 small onion, finely chopped

½ cup chopped fresh parsley

Salt

¼ teaspoon freshly ground black pepper

1. In a medium saucepan, bring water the to a boil, add the quinoa, and cover. Reduce the heat and let simmer for 15 minutes, or until the water has been absorbed. Remove the lid and let cool.

2. In a small bowl, combine the oil, lemon juice, and garlic. Stir to combine.

3. In a large bowl, add the smoked tofu, cucumber, red bell pepper, onion, and parsley. Pour the dressing over and stir.

4. Add the cooled quinoa and stir to combine.

5. Season with salt and pepper before serving.

TIP: *Some people are sensitive to quinoa's slight bitterness, which is the result of saponin, a naturally occurring chemical compound found in the ancient grain. Rinsing the quinoa before cooking can help reduce the bitterness.*

PREP TIME:
10 MINUTES

COOK TIME:
10 MINUTES

Mexican Black Bean Salad

The flavors in this Mexican-style salad are brightened up with the addition of a lime-based vinaigrette. Try serving it with a side of crunchy tortilla chips and, if you're feeling really festive, an icy-cold margarita.

To make the salad

In a large bowl, stir to combine all the salad ingredients. Be careful not to bruise the avocado.

To make the vinaigrette

In a small bowl, whisk together the lime juice, oil, cumin, salt, pepper, and Tabasco sauce (if using). Pour over the black bean mixture, and stir. Add the cilantro and stir again. Serve immediately.

For the salad

1 (15-ounce) can black beans, drained and rinsed

1 large tomato, washed and cut into dice

1 large green bell pepper, finely chopped

1 small jalapeño pepper, minced (optional)

1 small onion, minced

1 avocado, pitted, halved, and cubed

Corn kernels cut from ear of corn, or about ½ cup

For the vinaigrette

Juice of 1 lime

1 tablespoon extra-virgin olive oil

¼ teaspoon toasted cumin powder

Salt

Freshly ground black pepper

Dash Tabasco sauce (optional)

½ cup finely chopped fresh cilantro

Simple Orzo Salad

NUT-FREE
SOY-FREE
QUICK & EASY

PREP TIME:
10 MINUTES

COOK TIME:
10 MINUTES

Orzo looks a lot like rice but it's actually a tiny pasta variety that can be prepared much like any other pasta. This salad calls for chickpeas, but you could substitute red kidney beans or cannellini beans without compromising flavor.

For the salad

3 cups water

1 teaspoon salt

1 cup orzo

½ (15-ounce) can chickpeas, drained and rinsed (about ¾ cup)

1 large tomato, diced

1 small red onion, finely chopped

¼ cup finely chopped fresh basil leaves

¼ cup finely chopped Italian parsley

For the vinaigrette

1 tablespoon red wine vinegar

1 tablespoon extra-virgin olive oil

1 teaspoon agave nectar

Salt

Freshly ground black pepper

To make the salad

1. In a medium saucepan over medium-high heat, bring the water and salt to a boil and add the orzo. Stir, cover, and reduce the heat. Let simmer for 6 to 8 minutes, or until al dente. Drain, rinse, and cool.

2. In a large bowl, add the orzo, chickpeas, tomatoes, onion, basil, and parsley, and stir to combine.

To make the vinaigrette

1. In a small bowl, whisk together the vinegar, oil, and agave nectar. Season with salt and pepper. Pour over the orzo mixture and stir to combine.

2. Season with additional salt and pepper before serving the salad.

TOSS IT TOGETHER TIP: *Turn the remaining chickpeas into a crunchy appetizer. Toss with a bit of extra-virgin olive oil, salt, and cumin powder. Roast at 475°F for 15 minutes, or until crunchy. Eat fresh out of the oven.*

Summertime Panzanella

This classic Italian salad unites an unlikely combination: stale bread and luscious, juicy tomatoes. The flavors are simple and rustic but very satisfying. Serve with a glass of Chianti or another Italian wine to bring out the fresh flavors in the dish.

To make the salad

1. Preheat the oven to 475°F.

2. In the oven, roast the red bell pepper for 15 minutes, or until it collapses and the skin is blistered. Let cool, then peel, seed, and roughly chop.

3. In a large bowl, add the roasted pepper, tomatoes, capers, onion, basil, and bread cubes.

To make the vinaigrette

1. In a small bowl, whisk together the vinegar, oil, and garlic.

2. Pour the dressing over the salad. Season with salt and black pepper before serving the salad.

TIP: *Don't have any stale bread handy? Take a fresh baguette and cut it into large cubes, then toast in the oven on low heat for 20 minutes. You're not looking for a golden, toasty color; you just want to firm it up and give the bread a bit of bite.*

For the salad

1 large red bell pepper

2 large tomatoes, roughly chopped

1 tablespoon capers, rinsed and drained

1 small red onion, thinly sliced

¼ cup roughly chopped fresh basil

2 cups stale baguette, ciabatta, or other firm white bread, cut into large cubes

For the vinaigrette

1 tablespoon red wine vinegar

2 tablespoons extra-virgin olive oil

1 small garlic clove, minced

Salt

Freshly ground black pepper

Thai Peanut Slaw

The quintessential flavors of Thai cooking—chiles, mint, basil—are present in this easy-to-prepare dish, which makes a great lunch or a light supper on a warm day. If you have a peanut allergy, omit the peanut butter. The authentic flavors will still be in place, only the salad will have a lighter, less-filling feel.

For the slaw

2 cups thinly sliced
  red cabbage
½ large cucumber, peeled,
  seeded, and thinly sliced
1 carrot, washed and grated
1 small red onion, thinly sliced
1 small jalapeño pepper,
  thinly sliced
¼ cup finely chopped fresh
  mint leaves
¼ cup finely chopped fresh
  basil leaves
¼ cup finely chopped fresh
  cilantro leaves

For the dressing

2 tablespoons peanut butter
2 tablespoons coconut milk
2 teaspoons soy sauce
Juice of 1 lime
1 tablespoon agave nectar
½ teaspoon red chili paste
  (optional)

To make the slaw

In a large bowl, combine all of the ingredients for the slaw.

To make the dressing

1. In a small bowl, stir together the ingredients for the dressing. If the sauce is too thick to pour, add a bit more coconut milk or water to thin.

2. Pour the dressing over the cabbage mixture and stir to combine.

3. Serve immediately.

TOSS IT TOGETHER TIP: *Blend the remaining coconut milk into tomorrow morning's smoothie for a decadent start to the day. If the flavor is too rich, thin with a little juice, water, or non-dairy milk.*

Bok Choy–Sesame Salad

Not everyone knows that bok choy tastes delicious raw as well as cooked. To allow the flavors to meld and the bok choy to soften, let the salad sit for 15 minutes or more after adding the sesame dressing.

1. In a large bowl, combine the bok choy, onion, mushrooms, basil, and mint.

2. In a small bowl, whisk together the lime juice, sesame oil, and soy sauce.

3. Pour over the bok choy mixture. Season with black pepper and red pepper flakes (if using).

4. Let marinate for 15 minutes before serving.

TIP: *Dried shiitake mushrooms are a good staple to have in your pantry. They keep for up to a year if stored in a cool, dry container. They have a unique flavor that works well in Chinese, Japanese, and other Asian-inspired recipes.*

4 baby bok choy florets, washed, trimmed, and finely sliced

1 small red onion, thinly sliced

4 dried shiitake mushrooms, reconstituted in warm water and thinly sliced

¼ cup finely chopped fresh basil leaves

¼ cup finely chopped fresh mint leaves

Juice of 1 lime

1 teaspoon toasted sesame oil

1 tablespoon soy sauce or tamari

Freshly ground black pepper

Red pepper flakes (optional)

Warm Lentil-Mushroom Salad

There's something extra satisfying about a warm salad. This super simple recipe brings together the heartiness of lentils with the classic flavors of garlic, arugula, and lemon. This dish is best enjoyed right after it's prepared so that the arugula doesn't get soggy.

PREP TIME:
15 MINUTES

COOK TIME:
20 MINUTES

¾ cup du Puy lentils (also called "French" or "Beluga" lentils)

1 teaspoon herbes de Provence

2½ cups water

2 tablespoons extra-virgin olive oil, divided

2 cups thickly sliced cremini, portobello, or other firm mushroom

1 large garlic clove, minced

Red pepper flakes (optional)

1 tablespoon freshly squeezed lemon juice

Salt

Freshly ground black pepper

1 cup arugula

¼ cup finely chopped Italian parsley

1. In a large saucepan, combine the lentils, herbes de Provence, and water. Simmer, covered, for 20 minutes, or until the lentils are tender. Drain any excess water and let cool.

2. In a large nonstick skillet over medium-high heat, add 1 tablespoon oil. Sear the mushrooms until golden, about 15 minutes. Add the garlic and red pepper flakes (if using). Cook 1 minute more.

3. In a large bowl, toss the lentils and mushroom-garlic mixture together. Add the lemon juice and remaining 1 tablespoon oil. Season with salt and pepper. Stir.

4. Just before serving, stir in the arugula and parsley and stir to combine.

Barley-Butternut Salad

Barley is a wonderful grain that isn't as fashionable as some of the others out there (hello, quinoa!), but it deserves a regular rotation into your mealtime routine. This salad is full of autumn-harvest flavor, and fills you up without weighing you down.

To make the salad

1. Preheat the oven 450°F.

2. Place the squash and onions on a baking tray. Toss with the oil and sprinkle with salt. Roast until the squash is tender and the onions are soft and fragrant, about 20 minutes.

3. In a medium-size saucepan, combine the barley and water. Bring to a boil. Lower the heat, cover, and simmer for 25 minutes, or until the barley is tender. Drain if necessary and let cool.

4. In a large bowl, add the barley, squash-onion mixture, walnuts, parsley, and spinach. Stir to combine.

To make the dressing

In a small bowl, whisk together the vinegar, oil, and garlic. Pour the dressing over the barley-squash mixture, stir, and season with salt and pepper. Serve immediately.

For the salad

1 small butternut squash, peeled, seeded, and cut into small chunks

1 small red onion, thickly chopped

1 teaspoon extra-virgin olive oil

Salt

1 cup pearl barley

2 cups water

2 tablespoons roughly chopped toasted walnuts

¼ cup roughly chopped Italian parsley

1 cup baby spinach

For the dressing

1 tablespoon balsamic vinegar

2 tablespoons extra-virgin olive oil

1 garlic clove, minced

Salt

Freshly ground black pepper

Warm Potato and Smoked Tempeh Salad

Tempeh, a staple in Indonesian cooking, gives lots of meaty texture and the perfect bland base for almost any seasoning you can imagine. In this comfort-food dish, tempeh conspires with potatoes to tempt you into making enough for second helpings.

PREP TIME:
15 MINUTES

COOK TIME:
15 MINUTES

For the salad

3 cups red potatoes, cubed
1 tablespoon extra-virgin olive oil
1 small red onion, finely chopped
1 (8-ounce) package smoked tempeh, cut into large dice
¼ cup finely chopped Italian parsley
1 scallion, finely chopped

For the vinaigrette

1 tablespoon extra-virgin olive oil
2 tablespoons balsamic vinegar
1 tablespoon Dijon mustard
2 tablespoons maple syrup
Salt
Freshly ground black pepper

To make the salad

1. Wash the potatoes and steam them for 10 to 12 minutes, or until easily pierced with a fork. Drain and set aside.

2. In a nonstick skillet over medium-high heat, add the oil, onion, and tempeh. Sauté, stirring regularly, for 5 to 7 minutes, or until the tempeh is golden, and the onions are translucent.

3. In a large bowl, add the potatoes, tempeh-onion mixture, parsley, and scallion.

To make the vinaigrette

1. In a small bowl, whisk together the oil, vinegar, mustard, and maple syrup.

2. Pour the dressing over the salad, and stir to combine.

3. Season with salt and pepper. Serve immediately.

Creamy Kale Caesar

This updated twist on the classic Caesar pairs kale and avocado with a tangy tahini sauce that adds heft and flavor to this already nourishing salad. To make this meal-in-a-bowl even more filling, toss in some homemade croutons or a few of your favorite beans.

To make the salad

In a large bowl, combine all of the ingredients for the salad.

To make the Caesar dressing

1. In a small bowl, whisk together all of the ingredients. It should be thick but pourable. If it's too thick, add water a teaspoon at a time to reach the right consistency.

2. Pour the Caesar dressing over the kale mixture and toss to combine. Season generously with pepper, and salt as needed.

For the salad
4 cups thinly sliced kale
1 small red onion, thinly sliced
¼ cup thinly sliced black olives
1 avocado, diced

For the Caesar dressing
3 tablespoons tahini
    (sesame seed paste)
Juice of 1 lemon
2 teaspoons soy sauce
    or tamari
1 garlic clove, minced
2 tablespoons nutritional
    yeast flakes
Freshly ground black pepper
Salt

Crunchy Couscous Salad

Couscous salad is ideal for a weekday lunch. The longer the flavors are allowed to marry, the better, and it tastes equally good at room temperature as it does cold. Serve this right away, or pack it for tomorrow's mid-day meal at the office.

PREP TIME:
10 MINUTES

COOK TIME:
5 MINUTES

1¾ cups water

¼ cup raisins

⅓ teaspoon salt

2 tablespoons extra-virgin olive oil, divided

1 cup fine couscous

1 small red onion, finely chopped

1 red bell pepper, chopped into small dice

½ cucumber, peeled, seeded, and chopped into small dice

1 tablespoon capers, rinsed

¼ cup roughly chopped toasted almonds

¼ cup finely chopped cilantro, mint, or Italian parsley

Juice of 1 lemon

1 garlic clove, minced

Salt

Freshly ground black pepper

1. In a medium saucepan, add the water, raisins, salt, and 1 tablespoon oil. Bring to a boil. Stir in the couscous, and immediately remove from the heat.

2. Let stand, covered, for 5 minutes. Transfer to a large bowl and fluff with a fork. When cool, add the onion, bell pepper, cucumber, capers, almonds, and cilantro.

3. In a small bowl, whisk together the lemon juice, remaining 1 tablespoon oil, and garlic.

4. Pour over the couscous mixture. Stir to combine.

5. Season with salt and pepper, and serve.

QUICK & EASY
NUT-FREE

PREP TIME:
15 MINUTES

COOK TIME:
5 MINUTES

Buckwheat Soba Salad

Gluten-free buckwheat noodles form the foundation of this simple, tasty salad, and to keep their toothsome texture intact, take care not to overcook them. For the perfect al dente bite, rinse the noodles in a cold-water bath immediately after draining to remove excess starch and halt the cooking process.

To make the salad

In a large bowl, toss together all of the ingredients.

To make the vinaigrette

1. In a small saucepan over medium-high heat, add the ginger, garlic, sesame oil, soy sauce, vinegar, and sugar for the vinaigrette. Bring to a boil, then reduce the heat and simmer for 2 minutes. Remove from the heat and let cool slightly.

2. Pour the warm vinaigrette over the noodle-vegetable mixture and toss to combine. Sprinkle with the sesame seeds (if using) before serving.

For the salad

Cooked buckwheat noodles
  for two people
1 medium carrot, grated
1 small red bell pepper,
  cored and thinly sliced
2 scallions, thinly sliced

For the vinaigrette

½-inch piece fresh ginger,
  minced
1 small garlic clove, minced
1 teaspoon toasted sesame oil
1 tablespoon soy sauce
  or tamari
2 teaspoons rice wine vinegar
½ teaspoon sugar
Toasted sesame seeds, to
  garnish (optional)

Salad with Lentils, Chickpeas & Vegetables

SOY-FREE
NUT-FREE
GLUTEN-FREE

PREP TIME:
5 MINUTES

TOTAL TIME:
30 MINUTES

The only thing better than the way this salad tastes is the ease with which it comes together. When tossed with fresh veggies, your leftover rice (or other grain) gets a major flavor upgrade, and the flavors continue to improve the longer you let this salad sit.

For the salad

1 cup cooked rice or other grain (quinoa or farro would work well)

½ (15-ounce) can of chickpeas, rinsed and drained

1 cup cooked green beans, sliced lengthwise

1 small red onion, peeled and thinly sliced

5 cremini or other firm mushrooms, thinly sliced

3 sun-dried tomatoes packed in olive oil, sliced thinly

For the dressing

2 tablespoons olive oil

1 tablespoon red wine vinegar

½ teaspoon herbes de Provence

1 teaspoon salt

½ teaspoon sugar

1. In a large bowl, combine all the salad ingredients.

2. In a small jar, combine the dressing ingredients and shake vigorously until well-combined.

3. Pour the dressing over the salad mixture, toss to combine, and let sit for 20 minutes before serving.

SUPERB SIDES & ALLURING APPETIZERS

PREP TIME:
5 MINUTES

COOK TIME:
15 MINUTES

Garlicky Kale Crostini

This crunchy, earthy appetizer is delightful plated as a first course, and equally enticing when served alongside a main-meal salad or even your morning tofu scramble. To punch up the flavor a bit more, add a pinch of red pepper flakes to the kale as it cooks.

1. Preheat the oven to 400°F.

2. On a baking sheet, arrange the bread slices and brush with 2 teaspoons oil. Season with salt and pepper. Bake until light golden brown, about 7 minutes.

3. Remove from the oven to cool.

4. In a large nonstick skillet over medium-high heat, add the remaining 1 teaspoon oil and garlic. Sauté, stirring until the garlic just changes color, taking care not to overcook.

5. Add the kale and sauté, stirring, for 5 minutes.

6. Add the water, cover, and reduce heat, cooking for 5 minutes or until the water evaporates.

7. Remove from the heat, add the lemon juice, and season with salt and pepper.

8. To serve, top each slice of toasted baguette with a generous spoonful of kale.

TOSS IT TOGETHER TIP: *Baguettes go stale quickly, so consider turning the rest of your bread into longer-lasting croutons. Simply slice the bread, drizzle with a bit of extra-virgin olive oil and rub each slice with ½ clove of garlic, cut into cubes, and toast at 200°F for 10 minutes. Store in a glass jar in a cool, dry place for up to a week.*

TOSS IT TOGETHER TIP: *When a recipe calls for the juice of half of a lemon, you're left with a slew of tart and tangy possibilities for putting the other half to good use. Try it in place of vinegar in your next vinaigrette, squeeze it into a tall glass of water for a refreshing palate cleanser, or squeeze it over steamed beet greens or kale.*

½ baguette, thickly sliced (about 8 slices)

3 tablespoons extra-virgin olive oil, divided

Salt

Freshly ground black pepper

2 garlic cloves, minced

3 cups kale, destemmed and sliced into thin strips

½ cup water

Juice of ½ lemon

Robust Red-Pepper Hummus

This "hummus" doesn't contain chickpeas like the original, but it still has all the thick, flavorful qualities of its namesake. Serve as a spread for sandwiches, a dip for veggies, or a sauce for pasta.

PREP TIME:
10 MINUTES

COOK TIME:
15 MINUTES

1 large red bell pepper
2 baguette slices, cubed
(about ½ cup)
1 small garlic clove
¼ cup toasted walnut pieces
1 teaspoon smoked paprika
1 teaspoon balsamic vinegar
Juice of ½ lemon
1 teaspoon extra-virgin
olive oil
¼ cup water
Salt
Freshly ground black pepper

1. Preheat the oven to 475°F.

2. Roast the red pepper under the broiler for 10 minutes, turning halfway through to blacken each side. When the pepper is charred and the flesh has collapsed, remove from the oven and allow to cool before peeling and removing the stem and seeds.

3. On a baking sheet, toast the baguette cubes in the oven until golden, about 3 to 5 minutes.

4. In a food processor, add the garlic and walnuts. Process for 10 seconds.

5. Add the roasted pepper, toasted baguette cubes, and paprika. Process until smooth, about 10 seconds.

6. Add the vinegar, lemon juice, oil, water, and salt and pepper to taste. Pulse until well blended. If the mixture is too thick, add a bit more water to thin.

7. Let sit for an hour or more before serving to allow flavors to develop.

PREP TIME:
5 MINUTES

COOK TIME:
25 MINUTES

Cauliflower Buffalo Wings

You'll find neither buffalo nor wings of any kind in this dish. The "buffalo" is code for "hot sauce," and Tabasco or another spicy sauce will do the trick. If you do find "buffalo" sauce at the supermarket, check the label to ensure it doesn't contain butter.

1. Preheat the oven to 450°F.

2. In a large bowl, combine the water, flour, garlic powder, salt and pepper to taste. Whisk to combine. Add the cauliflower florets. Toss with a spoon to coat each piece in the flour mixture.

3. On a baking sheet, spread the cauliflower florets and bake for 15 minutes, then remove from the oven.

4. In a small bowl, combine the hot sauce and vegan margarine. Spoon over the cauliflower, and return to the oven to bake for 10 more minutes.

5. Serve hot with your favorite dipping sauce.

TIP: *Are you sensitive to wheat? Use your favorite gluten-free flour— garbanzo bean, rice, sorghum—or flour blend without losing any flavor or texture of the original recipe.*

½ cup water or soy milk
½ cup all-purpose flour
1 teaspoon garlic powder
Salt
Freshly ground black pepper
3 cups cauliflower florets (roughly ½ head of cauliflower), washed and dried
½ cup hot sauce
2 teaspoons vegan margarine, melted

Smoky Cashew Cheese

This fast-and-easy cheese is made with agar-agar, a seaweed-derived gelatin that's totally suitable for vegans, and completely easy to master. Make this two or three times and you'll be a pro! Serve it with crusty bread and a bowl of olives for a tasty appetizer.

PREP TIME:
10 MINUTES

COOK TIME:
5 MINUTES

1½ cups water
1 teaspoon salt
1 teaspoon garlic powder
2 teaspoons agar-agar powder
¾ cup raw cashews, soaked for three hours (or overnight), drained, and rinsed
¼ cup nutritional yeast
1 teaspoon smoked paprika
Juice of ½ lemon

1. In a medium saucepan over medium heat, combine the water, salt, garlic powder, and agar-agar powder. Simmer, whisking, until thickened and the agar is fully dissolved, about 5 minutes.

2. Remove from the heat.

3. In a medium-size bowl, add the cashews, nutritional yeast, paprika, and lemon juice.

4. Add the warm agar mixture, and using an immersion or standard blender, blend until smooth.

5. Pour into a lightly oiled mold or small bowl. Allow to cool before unmolding and slicing.

TOSS IT TOGETHER TIP: *Besides making a great addition to your hors d'oeuvres platter, this cheese can be grated over casseroles, stuffed inside tacos, or sliced into sandwiches.*

PREP TIME:
10 MINUTES

COOK TIME:
15 MINUTES

Saucy Tahini Broccoli

Broccoli gets a next-level flavor boost from this simple sauce made with a rich, creamy sesame-seed paste known as tahini. The sauce can also be used as a salad dressing or a sauce for rice or noodles, and tastes better the next day.

To make the broccoli

1. Preheat the oven to 450°F.

2. In a large bowl, add the broccoli, oil, and red pepper flakes (if using). Season with salt and pepper.

3. On a baking sheet, add the broccoli florets and roast for 15 minutes, turning once. The broccoli should be tender and lightly browned.

To make the sauce

1. In a small bowl, add the garlic, tahini, lemon juice, and water. Whisk until well blended. Season with salt and pepper.

2. To serve, plate the broccoli and drizzle with the tahini sauce.

For the broccoli

3 cups broccoli florets, washed and dried

1 tablespoon extra-virgin olive oil

Pinch red pepper flakes (optional)

Salt

Freshly ground black pepper

For the sauce

1 small garlic clove, minced

3 tablespoons tahini

Juice of 1 lemon

2 tablespoons water

Salt

Freshly ground black pepper

Miso-Glazed Butternut Squash

While this recipe is made with the colorful, easy-to-find butternut squash, you could easily substitute kabocha, acorn, or another squash variety. This dish wouldn't be out of place on a Thanksgiving table, but can also be cooled, chopped, and served in a spinach salad.

PREP TIME:
10 MINUTES

COOK TIME:
30 MINUTES

1 small butternut squash, peeled, seeded, and cut into thick wedges

3 teaspoons sesame oil, divided

Salt

1 tablespoon miso paste

2 tablespoons water

1 tablespoon maple syrup

1. Preheat the oven to 425°F.

2. In a large bowl, add the squash wedges. Drizzle with 1 teaspoon sesame oil and toss to coat. Season with salt and arrange the wedges on a cookie sheet. Bake for 20 minutes or until just tender, turning once.

3. In a small saucepan over medium heat, combine the miso paste, water, maple syrup, and remaining 2 teaspoons sesame oil. Simmer, stirring, until the miso dissolves.

4. Spoon the miso glaze over the squash wedges and return to the oven.

5. Bake for 10 minutes more before serving.

TIP: *The fermented soybean paste known as miso is extremely versatile and comes in multiple varieties. Try the mellow white miso, which has a mild, salty-sweet flavor that adapts well to sauces, dips, and soups.*

PREP TIME:
5 MINUTES

COOK TIME:
10 MINUTES

Hoisin Green Beans

This side dish makes a tasty accompaniment to Asian-inspired mains, and can be made into a one-pot meal with the addition of some cubed tofu and cooked noodles. For the best cooking results, use an oil with a low smoke point, such as coconut or canola.

1. In a medium-size nonstick skillet over medium-high heat, add the oil and green beans and sauté, stirring, for 3 minutes. Add the garlic. Sauté, stirring, for 3 minutes more, or until the garlic is golden.

2. Add the hoisin sauce and water. Cook, stirring, until the beans are tender, about 2 minutes. To serve, season with salt and red pepper flakes.

TOSS IT TOGETHER TIP: *Not sure what to do with the rest of your jar of hoisin sauce? Blend it with your favorite barbecue sauce before grilling. Use it as a simmer sauce or marinade for tofu or tempeh. Blend it with Sriracha and use it as a spicy dip for roasted potatoes.*

2 teaspoons coconut, canola, or extra-virgin olive oil

3 cups fresh green beans, trimmed and sliced in half

2 garlic cloves, finely chopped

2 tablespoons hoisin sauce

2 tablespoons water

Salt

Red pepper flakes

Roasted Brussels Sprouts

GLUTEN-FREE
NUT-FREE
SOY-FREE

PREP TIME:
10 MINUTES

COOK TIME:
30 MINUTES

This simple recipe brings out the Brussels sprouts' inherent sweetness and eliminates any bitterness. Serve these little gems alongside a giant scoop of mashed potatoes and Miso-Glazed Butternut Squash (page 67) for a flavorful, colorful autumn-harvest meal.

3 cups Brussels sprouts, trimmed and sliced into quarters

1 tablespoon extra-virgin olive oil

1 garlic clove, finely chopped

½ teaspoon salt

Pinch red pepper flakes (optional)

Freshly ground black pepper

1. Preheat the oven to 400°F.

2. In a large bowl, add the Brussels sprouts. Toss with the oil, garlic, salt, and red pepper flakes.

3. Pour the Brussels sprouts onto a baking sheet and roast for 30 minutes, until golden on the outside and tender on the inside.

4. To serve, season with additional salt and black pepper.

Cumin-Roasted Carrots

PREP TIME:
5 MINUTES

COOK TIME:
40 MINUTES

Cumin and carrots are a match made in culinary heaven. The flavors recall the cooking traditions of North African countries, and marry well with other foods from that part of the world, including couscous and chickpeas.

1. Preheat the oven to 400°F.

2. In a large bowl, combine the carrots, oil, cumin seeds, and salt. Toss to coat.

3. Pour the carrots onto a baking sheet and roast until lightly caramelized and tender, 35 to 40 minutes, turning once.

4. Serve warm.

4 large carrots, washed, peeled, and cut into ½-inch chunks

1½ teaspoons extra-virgin olive oil

½ teaspoon cumin seeds

½ teaspoon salt

TIP: *These carrots can be served cold and make a great addition to a Mediterranean mezze platter alongside a couscous salad and Chermoula-Spiced Eggplant (page 73).*

Twice-Cooked Plantains

GLUTEN-FREE
NUT-FREE
SOY-FREE

Plantains are a starchier, less-sweet relative of the banana. Raw, they have the consistency of an underripe banana, and when cooked, they're more akin to a potato. Serve these alongside rice and black beans for an authentic Latin American experience.

PREP TIME:
10 MINUTES

COOK TIME:
25 MINUTES

1 large green plantain, peeled and cut into roughly 10 diagonal slices

1 tablespoon extra-virgin olive oil, divided

1 teaspoon garlic powder

1 teaspoon chili powder

Salt

1. Preheat the oven to 425°F.

2. In a medium-size bowl, add the plantain slices, 1 teaspoon oil, garlic powder, chili powder, and salt, to taste. Stir to coat the plantains in the oil and spice mixture.

3. In a large nonstick skillet over medium-high heat, add the remaining 2 teaspoons oil. Fry the plantains until golden, about 3 minutes per side. Remove from heat and transfer plantains to a baking sheet.

4. Using the bottom of a heavy glass or mug, flatten each plantain slice so that it almost doubles in circumference. Bake in the oven for 15 minutes, or until crispy on the outside, and soft on the inside.

5. Serve hot with your favorite dipping sauce.

Zucchini Fritters

PREP TIME:
10 MINUTES

COOK TIME:
10 MINUTES

If you have friends who garden, you've probably found yourself in possession of at least one impressively large, but utterly flavorless zucchini. This recipe is perfect for that squash. When fried and lightly seasoned, zucchini goes from bland to mouthwatering.

1. On a clean tea towel inside a colander, add the zucchini and sprinkle with salt. Let sit for 10 minutes, then squeeze to remove as much moisture as possible.

2. In a small bowl, add the flaxseed and water. Stir to combine. Let thicken for 5 minutes.

3. In a medium-size bowl, add the zucchini, flaxseed mixture, onion, garlic, flour, and oregano (if using). Stir to combine, then form into six patties.

4. In a large nonstick skillet over medium-high heat, add the oil and the zucchini patties. Fry for 3 to 4 minutes, or until golden. Flip and cook for 3 minutes more.

5. Serve with your favorite dipping sauce and a squeeze of lemon.

1 large zucchini, washed and grated
½ teaspoon salt
1 tablespoon flaxseed
2 tablespoons water
1 small onion, thinly sliced
1 garlic clove, minced
2 tablespoons all-purpose flour
Pinch oregano (optional)
1 tablespoon coconut or canola oil
Lemon wedges, for garnish

Chermoula-Spiced Eggplant

Chermoula is an enticing blend of pungent, tangy spices from North Africa that is often used as a rub for grilling. Here, it gives eggplant a seductive flavor overhaul, making lovers out of even ardent eggplant naysayers. The sauce can be made a day ahead for easy preparation.

SOY-FREE
NUT-FREE

PREP TIME:
10 MINUTES

COOK TIME:
30 MINUTES

1 medium eggplant, cut into ½-inch rounds

1½ teaspoons salt, divided

1 garlic clove, minced

1 teaspoon smoked paprika

½ teaspoon cumin powder

¼ cup finely chopped cilantro, divided

¼ cup finely chopped parsley, divided

Juice of 1 lemon

2 tablespoons extra-virgin olive oil, divided

1. Preheat the oven to 350°F.

2. On a tea towel, spread the eggplant slices and sprinkle both sides with ½ teaspoon salt. Let sit for 20 minutes, then pat dry.

3. In a medium bowl, toss together the garlic, paprika, cumin, 2 tablespoons cilantro and 2 tablespoons parsley, lemon juice, 1 tablespoon oil, and ½ teaspoon salt. Stir to combine.

4. On a lightly oiled baking sheet, arrange the eggplant slices and bake for 20 to 30 minutes, or until tender. Remove from the oven and let cool.

5. In a medium-size nonstick skillet over medium-high heat, add the remaining 1 tablespoon oil and fry the eggplant two or three at a time until crispy and golden.

6. To serve, stir the chermoula sauce again and spoon it over the eggplant slices.

7. Top with the remaining 2 tablespoons cilantro and remaining 2 tablespoons parsley, season with the remaining ½ teaspoon salt, and let sit for 20 minutes before serving.

TOSS IT TOGETHER TIP: *If you find yourself with a little extra chermoula sauce on your hands, use it as a marinade for tofu, tempeh, or any other treat you intend to toss on the grill. It also makes an interesting dipping sauce for bread.*

GLUTEN-FREE
NUT-FREE
QUICK & EASY

PREP TIME:
10 MINUTES

COOK TIME:
20 MINUTES

Magically Good Mushroom Pâté

This pâté is easy to make once you get the hang of it. You can eat it as an appetizer, a sandwich spread, or even the main course with a side of mashed potatoes and a green salad. Try doubling the quantity and bringing it to your next food-centric gathering.

1. In a medium-size nonstick skillet over medium heat, add the oil and onions, stirring occasionally, until the onions are translucent, about 4 minutes. Add the garlic and sauté 1 minute more. Add the mushrooms, herbes de Provence, salt, and pepper to taste. Sauté until the mushrooms soften and brown slightly, about 5 minutes.

2. Add the red wine, nutritional yeast, miso, and potato. Stir to combine, then simmer for 2 minutes. Add the agar-water mixture, stir, and let simmer for 5 minutes more.

3. Remove from the heat.

4. Using an immersion blender, purée the mixture while still warm.

5. In a lightly oiled mold, add the mushroom mixture.

6. Cool for 20 minutes in the refrigerator before serving.

2 teaspoons extra-virgin olive oil

½ cup finely chopped onion

1 garlic clove, minced

3 cups roughly chopped cremini, portobello, or other firm mushroom

½ teaspoon herbes de Provence

½ teaspoon salt

Freshly ground black pepper

¼ cup red wine

2 tablespoons nutritional yeast

1 tablespoon miso paste

1 medium waxy potato, peeled, steamed, cooled, and roughly chopped

2 teaspoons agar-agar powder, dissolved in ½ cup water

Roman Holiday Artichokes

Artichokes are not only delicious, but they're full of nutrients that support digestion and liver function. Choose 'chokes with green stems, and prevent unsightly discoloration while you prep your meal by tossing them in a bowl of cold water with a generous squeeze of lemon added.

PREP TIME:
10 MINUTES

COOK TIME:
30 MINUTES

¼ cup finely chopped parsley

2 garlic cloves, finely chopped

1 teaspoon salt

2 teaspoons extra-virgin olive oil

2 large artichokes, washed and trimmed, halved lengthwise, and fuzzy chokes removed

½ cup white wine

½ cup boiling water

1. Preheat the oven to 450°F.

2. In a small bowl, combine the parsley, garlic, salt, and oil.

3. Place the artichokes in a lightly oiled baking pan. Spoon a dollop of the parsley mixture into each artichoke half.

4. Slowly pour the wine and water into the baking dish, taking care not to splash the tops of the artichokes.

5. Cover and bake for 20 to 30 minutes.

6. Let cool slightly before serving.

Beet Tartare

PREP TIME:
5 MINUTES

COOK TIME:
20 MINUTES

Beets offer a good dose of vitamin C and fiber in every bite, and this dish has the added benefit of complex flavor, texture, and color. Red beets are one option; you could also prepare this French-inspired tartare with golden beets or the striped Chioggia variety.

1. In a large bowl, add the beets, lemon juice, lemon zest, 1 teaspoon oil, salt, and pepper to taste. Let sit for 1 hour to allow the flavors to marry.

2. Strain off the liquid from the beets. In the same bowl, add the onion, paprika, cumin, and remaining 2 teaspoons oil. Stir to combine.

3. To serve, sprinkle with the parsley. Season with additional salt and pepper.

TIP: *To give this dish a bit of sophistication while plating, spoon the beets into a circular mold or ring, press into shape, lift and remove, then serve.*

4 medium beets, steamed for 20 minutes or until tender and chopped into small dice

2 teaspoons freshly squeezed lemon juice

Zest of 1 lemon

1 tablespoon extra-virgin olive oil, divided

½ teaspoon salt

Freshly ground black pepper

1 small onion, minced

⅛ teaspoon smoked paprika

⅛ teaspoon ground cumin

2 tablespoons chopped Italian parsley

Spicy Vegetables

Asian flavors punctuate this hearty side dish that gets its heft from savory tempeh. Fresh ginger and garlic liven up the healthy cruciferous veggies that star in this recipe, while sliced green onions lend just the right amount of freshness.

PREP TIME:
10 MINUTES

COOK TIME:
10 MINUTES

2 teaspoons sesame oil

2 cloves garlic, thinly sliced

½-inch piece fresh ginger, minced

2 cups broccoli florets, washed

½ cup red cabbage, thinly sliced

½ (8-ounce) package tempeh, sliced into thin strips

½ teaspoon red pepper flakes

2 tablespoons soy sauce or wheat-free tamari, blended with 2 tablespoons water

1 green onion, washed and thinly sliced

1. In a medium non-stick skillet or wok over medium-high heat, add the sesame oil, garlic, and ginger. Cook, stirring, for 1 minute.

2. Add the broccoli, cabbage, and tempeh, and cook for 3 minutes more, stirring constantly.

3. Add the red pepper flakes and soy sauce–water mixture and stir. Cover and lower the heat, and allow to cook for 5 minutes, or until the broccoli and cabbage are tender and the liquid is evaporated.

4. Sprinkle with the green onion slices before serving.

STELLAR SOUPS & STEWS

Velvety Butternut Potage

PREP TIME:
10 MINUTES

COOK TIME:
30 MINUTES

This soup could be described as "comfort in a bowl." Smooth, soothing, and lightly spiced, it takes the edge off a cold day and gives a burst of color and flavor with every spoonful. If you don't have coconut milk on hand, replace with a cup of your favorite non-dairy milk, such as almond or rice.

1. In a medium saucepan over medium heat, add the oil, onion, garlic, and curry powder. Sauté, stirring, for 2 minutes. Add the squash and sauté 3 minutes more.

2. Add the water, and bring to a boil. Reduce the heat and simmer for 15 to 20 minutes, or until the squash is tender.

3. Add the coconut milk, salt, and sugar (if using). Let simmer 5 minutes.

4. Remove from the heat, and using an immersion or standard blender, purée the soup until smooth.

5. Serve warm with the saffron threads as garnish.

1 teaspoon extra-virgin olive oil

1 small onion, finely chopped

2 garlic cloves, chopped

1 teaspoon curry powder or paste

1 small butternut squash, peeled, seeded, and cubed

2 cups water

1 (5.5-ounce) can coconut milk

1 teaspoon salt

1 teaspoon sugar (optional)

¼ teaspoon saffron threads, for garnish (optional)

Creamy Carrot Bisque

The warming spices that give this savory bisque its signature flavor are often reserved for sweet preparations. Here, the cinnamon, ginger, and cloves enhance the carrots' innate sugariness and add a wonderful depth. Serve with warm slices of wholesome bread to round out the meal.

PREP TIME:
5 MINUTES

COOK TIME:
25 MINUTES

1 teaspoon extra-virgin olive oil
2 garlic cloves, finely chopped
1 small onion, chopped
1-inch piece fresh ginger, peeled and grated
4 large carrots, chopped into 1-inch chunks
1 small potato, peeled and cubed
3½ cups water
3 whole cloves
Pinch ground cinnamon
½ teaspoon salt
Freshly ground black pepper

1. In a medium saucepan over medium heat, add the oil, garlic, onions, and ginger. Sauté, stirring, for 5 minutes.

2. Add the carrots, potato, water, cloves, cinnamon, and salt. Simmer, covered, for 15 to 20 minutes, or until the carrots are tender.

3. Remove from the heat.

4. Using a spoon, remove the cloves and discard. Using an immersion blender or standard blender, purée the remaining soup. Return to the pot, heat through, sprinkle with pepper, and serve.

TOSS IT TOGETHER TIP: *Did you know that carrot greens are edible and delicious? Wash them, chop them up, and toss them into your next pot of vegetable soup or pasta sauce. They can also be transformed into a delicious pesto with the help of extra-virgin olive oil and garlic.*

Curried Cauliflower Soup

PREP TIME:
10 MINUTES

COOK TIME:
25 MINUTES

This lightly spiced soup is *almost* as satisfying as a trip to the Taj Mahal. For extra richness, add a dollop of plain, dairy-free yogurt after ladling into bowls, and serve with crunchy toasted pappadums or whole-wheat chapati.

1. In a medium saucepan over medium-high heat, add the oil and mustard seeds. When they begin to pop, add the onion, garlic, and curry powder. Sauté for 2 minutes.

2. Add the cauliflower, water, salt, and tomato paste. Simmer, covered, for 20 minutes, or until the cauliflower is tender.

3. Using an immersion or standard blender, purée the cauliflower mixture. Before serving, stir in the lemon juice and cilantro.

TIP: *Mustard seeds come in several varieties, the most common being black and yellow. They are interchangeable in most Indian-inspired dishes, though the black variety's flavor is slightly more pungent and makes a tastier impact.*

1 teaspoon extra-virgin olive oil
½ teaspoon mustard seeds
1 small onion, chopped
1 garlic clove, minced
1 teaspoon curry powder
½ cauliflower head, chopped
3 cups water
1 teaspoon salt
1 tablespoon tomato paste
Juice of 1 lemon
¼ cup finely chopped cilantro

Smoky Potato-Kale Soup

GLUTEN-FREE
SOY-FREE
NUT-FREE

PREP TIME:
10 MINUTES

COOK TIME:
35 MINUTES

This soup can be served two ways: Chunky-style as illustrated here, or puréed until smooth. Either method yields delicious results that are best enjoyed between bites of homemade garlic bread.

1 teaspoon extra-virgin olive oil

1 large onion, peeled and chopped

2 garlic cloves, minced

1 teaspoon smoked paprika

3½ cups water

1 large potato, peeled and cubed

1 (15-ounce) can cannellini beans

1 teaspoon salt

2 cups roughly chopped kale

Freshly ground black pepper

1. In a medium saucepan over medium-high heat, add the oil and onion. Sauté, stirring, for 3 minutes.

2. Add the garlic and paprika. Sauté for 1 minute more.

3. Add the water, potato, beans, and salt. Bring to a boil, reduce heat, and simmer, covered, for 20 minutes.

4. Add the kale and simmer, uncovered, for 10 minutes more.

5. To serve, ladle into bowls and dust with pepper.

PREP TIME:
10 MINUTES

COOK TIME:
40 MINUTES

Roasted Corn Chowder

This corn chowder tastes best when prepared with fresh corn kernels, but can also be made with the canned or frozen variety. If choosing canned corn, look for brands without added sugar.

1. Preheat the oven to 450°F.

2. In a small bowl, combine ½ teaspoon oil, corn, jalapeño pepper, and red bell pepper. Stir to coat with oil.

3. On a baking sheet, spread the corn-pepper mixture and roast in the oven for 15 minutes, turning once. Remove from oven and set aside.

4. In a medium saucepan over medium heat, add the remaining ½ teaspoon oil, onion, and garlic. Sauté for 3 minutes.

5. Add the potato, water, and salt. Simmer for 15 minutes, or until the potato is tender. Remove from the heat.

6. Add the corn-pepper mixture and milk. Using an immersion or standard blender, purée the mixture, leaving a few chunks for texture. Return to the heat and simmer for 3 minutes. To serve, season with pepper.

TIP: *An immersion blender is a must-have appliance in every home-cook's kitchen. It makes the task of puréeing soups and sauces nearly hassle-free. Many immersion blenders are sold with extra attachments for chopping, whipping, and grinding small quantities.*

1 teaspoon extra-virgin olive oil, divided

2 cups canned or fresh corn kernels

1 jalapeño pepper, seeded and chopped

1 red bell pepper, seeded and roughly chopped

1 large onion, peeled and chopped

2 garlic cloves, minced

1 large potato, peeled and cubed

2½ cups water

1 teaspoon salt

1 cup soy or coconut milk

Freshly ground black pepper

Amazing Minestrone

This simple, nourishing, and utterly delicious minestrone is easy to throw together and adaptable to different ingredients. Try subbing another green for the spinach—chard or kale would work well—and du Puy lentils in place of the beans. Soy curls would add even more bite to this toothsome soup.

PREP TIME:
10 MINUTES

COOK TIME:
25 MINUTES

1 teaspoon extra-virgin
   olive oil
1 small onion, diced
2 garlic cloves, minced
1 teaspoon herbes de Provence
3 tablespoons tomato paste
3½ cups water
1 large carrot, chopped into
   small chunks
1 potato, cut into small chunks
1 teaspoon salt
1 cup uncooked macaroni or
   other small pasta
½ (15-ounce) can kidney or
   cannellini beans
2 cups chopped spinach
Freshly ground black pepper

1. In a large saucepan over medium heat, add the oil, onion, garlic, and herbes de Provence. Sauté, stirring, for 3 minutes. Add the tomato paste, water, carrot, potato, and salt. Stir to combine and bring to a boil.

2. Add the uncooked pasta and beans.

3. Reduce the heat and simmer, covered, for 20 minutes.

4. Five minutes before serving, add the spinach and pepper.

TOSS IT TOGETHER TIP: *Turn the leftover beans into an easy spread for bread. Just toss them in a food processor with the juice of half a lemon, a pinch of salt, a clove of garlic, and a splash of extra-virgin olive oil.*

Mushroom-Barley Soup with Sage

PREP TIME:
10 MINUTES

COOK TIME:
35 MINUTES

Barley is an underappreciated grain that deserves its moment in the spotlight. Besides being pleasant-tasting and full of fiber, it's a good source of magnesium, iron, and vitamin B_6. For a more nutrient-dense soup, use hulled barley.

1. In a medium saucepan over medium heat, add the oil, onions, carrot, celery, mushrooms, and sage. Sauté for 5 minutes, stirring.

2. Add the barley, water, and bay leaf. Bring to a boil. Reduce the heat and simmer, covered, for 25 to 30 minutes, giving the pot a stir every 10 minutes.

3. Remove the lid, and add salt and pepper to taste.

4. Test the barley for doneness; if it's soft and chewy, the soup is ready.

1 teaspoon extra-virgin olive oil

1 small onion, finely chopped

1 medium carrot, diced

2 celery stalks, diced

10 cremini or other firm mushrooms, thickly sliced

¼ teaspoon dried sage

½ cup pearl barley

4 cups water

1 bay leaf

1 teaspoon salt

Freshly ground black pepper

Chickpea-Chard Stew

GLUTEN-FREE
NUT-FREE
SOY-FREE

PREP TIME:
10 MINUTES

COOK TIME:
30 MINUTES

Like its trendy green cousin kale, chard is a nutritional powerhouse that happens to taste delicious. The leaves are tender but the stalks can be tough; slice off the bottom inch or two for most recipes, and save the discarded bits for a homemade vegetable broth.

1 teaspoon extra-virgin
    olive oil
1 small onion, chopped
2 garlic cloves, finely chopped
1 teaspoon smoked paprika
1 (15-ounce) can chickpeas
3 cups finely chopped chard
    leaves and stems
3 cups water
2 large tomatoes, roughly
    chopped
¼ cup finely chopped Italian
    parsley
Juice from lemon wedges
Salt
Freshly ground black pepper

1. In a large saucepan over medium heat, add the oil, onion, garlic, and paprika. Sauté, stirring, for 3 minutes. Add the chickpeas. Sauté, stirring, for 3 more minutes.

2. Add the chard and sauté, stirring, for 3 minutes. Add the water and tomatoes. Stir to combine. Lower the heat and simmer, covered, for 20 minutes.

3. Stir in the parsley, ladle into bowls, and squeeze lemon juice over each one. Season with salt and pepper. Serve warm.

Sublime Split Pea Soup

PREP TIME:
10 MINUTES

COOK TIME:
40 MINUTES

This creamy soup gets its subtle, smoky flavor from smoked paprika, and a slight kick from the addition of a chile pepper. Yellow or green split peas are interchangeable in this recipe; they are nearly identical in flavor and texture, and both are good sources of protein.

1. In a medium saucepan over medium heat, add the oil, onion, garlic, and paprika. Sauté, stirring, for 3 minutes. Add the carrot and jalapeño. Sauté, stirring, for 3 more minutes.

2. Add the split peas and water. Stir. Bring to a boil, cover, and reduce the heat. Let simmer 30 minutes, then stir in the salt.

3. Using an immersion or standard blender, purée the soup and return to the heat. Warm through and serve.

TIP: *If the mere mention of the word "jalapeño" makes you break out into a sweat, substitute a mild Anaheim chile or even a green bell pepper to kick the heat right out of this recipe. The flavor will remain intact, and the kids will enjoy it, too.*

1 teaspoon extra-virgin olive oil
1 small onion, chopped
2 garlic cloves, finely chopped
1 teaspoon smoked paprika
1 carrot, finely chopped
1 jalapeño, poblano, or other hot green pepper, seeded and finely chopped
1½ cups dried split peas
4 cups water
1 teaspoon salt

Tunisian Red Lentil Soup

GLUTEN-FREE
NUT-FREE
SOY-FREE

PREP TIME:
10 MINUTES

COOK TIME:
35 MINUTES

Red lentils change color when cooking, mellowing to a deep yellow. However, the chili powder and smoked paprika in this recipe help keep this soup's color palette as rich as the soup itself. Look for the red lentils in Indian markets, where it is sometimes called "masoor dal."

1 teaspoon extra-virgin
   olive oil
1 small onion, finely chopped
2 garlic cloves, minced
1 teaspoon cumin powder
1 teaspoon chili powder
1 teaspoon smoked paprika
½ teaspoon ground cinnamon
1 teaspoon salt
Freshly ground black pepper
1½ cups red lentils
   (sometimes called
   coral lentils)
3½ cups water
2 large tomatoes, finely
   chopped
½ cup finely chopped cilantro
Lemon wedges, for garnish

1. In a medium saucepan over medium-high heat, add the oil and onion. Sauté for 3 minutes. Add the garlic, cumin, chili powder, paprika, cinnamon, salt, and pepper to taste. Cook for another minute.

2. Add the lentils, water, and tomatoes. Bring to a boil. Cover, reduce the heat, and cook for 30 minutes, stirring once or twice.

3. Remove from the heat and stir in the cilantro.

4. To serve, squeeze a lemon wedge over the soup and season with pepper.

PREP TIME:
10 MINUTES

COOK TIME:
35 MINUTES

Dill-icious Beet Borscht

This root-vegetable soup has an alluring ruby-red hue, and tastes as good cold as it does straight out of the pot. The optional dill pickle garnish adds complexity and crunch, and a tangy burst of flavor with every spoonful.

1. In a medium saucepan over medium heat, add the oil and onion. Sauté for 3 minutes, stirring.

2. Add the garlic, beets, carrot, potato, bay leaf, and water. Bring to a boil, cover, and reduce the heat. Let simmer for 20 minutes.

3. Add the dill, salt, and pepper to taste. Simmer 10 minutes more and remove from the heat.

4. To serve, ladle into bowls and garnish with a heaping teaspoon of chopped dill pickle (if using).

TIP: *If you bought beets with their greens intact, try adding a cup or two of cleaned, chopped leaves and stems to the soup while it simmers. It will increase the soup's nutritional value and add flavor, too.*

1 teaspoon extra-virgin olive oil

1 small onion, finely chopped

1 garlic clove, quartered

2 large beets, peeled and cut into dice

1 carrot, cut into small dice

1 medium potato, peeled and cut into small dice

1 bay leaf

4 cups water

¼ cup finely chopped fresh dill

1 teaspoon salt

Freshly ground black pepper

1 dill pickle, roughly chopped (optional)

Hearty Miso Stew

NUT-FREE

QUICK & EASY

PREP TIME:
10 MINUTES

COOK TIME:
20 MINUTES

Miso is a naturally fermented paste made from soy that sometimes includes grains such as barley or rice. It is full of beneficial bacteria that support digestion. To reap its benefits, only heat your miso until it reaches a gentle simmer. Boiling kills the bacteria, but won't affect the flavor of the broth.

3½ cups water

½-inch fresh ginger piece, peeled and cut into thin coins

2 garlic cloves, thinly sliced

1 small onion, thinly sliced

5 mushrooms, thinly sliced

1 small potato, peeled and thinly sliced

1 small carrot, thinly sliced

3 tablespoons miso paste

1 cup roughly chopped spinach

1 teaspoon sesame oil (optional)

1 scallion, thinly sliced

1. In a medium saucepan over medium-high heat, combine the water, ginger, garlic, onion, mushrooms, potato, and carrot. Bring to a boil. Reduce the heat and simmer for 20 minutes, or until the carrots are tender.

2. In a mug, add the miso and ladle in enough of the hot soup broth to dissolve the paste. When the miso is dissolved, pour the broth mixture back in the pot.

3. Add the spinach and remove from the heat.

4. To serve, ladle into bowls, drizzle with the sesame oil, and top with scallions.

Sesame-Soba Noodle Soup

PREP TIME:
10 MINUTES

COOK TIME:
15 MINUTES

Soba noodles are made with buckwheat flour, which—contrary to its name—is not related to wheat at all. Serve this gluten-free soup with a homemade *maki* roll and a side of pickled ginger for a light yet filling Japanese-inspired meal.

1. In a medium saucepan over medium heat, add the sesame oil, garlic, mushrooms, and ginger. Sauté, stirring, for 3 minutes.

2. Add the water and soy sauce. Bring to a boil, add the noodles, and reduce the heat. Simmer 5 minutes.

3. Add the spinach and scallions.

4. Let simmer 2 minutes more, then serve.

TIP: *Dried shiitake mushrooms work well in this recipe. First, soak the mushrooms in hot water for an hour, then remove and thinly slice as you would fresh mushrooms. Reserve the soaking liquid; its potent flavor will help season the soup broth.*

1 teaspoon sesame oil

1 garlic clove, minced

4 shiitake or other mushrooms, thinly sliced

1-inch piece fresh ginger, peeled and thinly sliced

3 cups water

3 tablespoons soy sauce or tamari

4 ounces buckwheat noodles

1 cup roughly chopped spinach

2 scallions, thinly sliced

Fab Faux Pho

This classic Vietnamese soup—phonetically named after the French word for fire, or *feu*—brims with bright flavor. What sets this noodle soup apart from others are the optional add-ins, including freshly squeezed lime juice and spicy jalapeños. To make this gluten-free, opt for a wheat-free tamari instead of soy sauce.

PREP TIME:
5 MINUTES

COOK TIME:
25 MINUTES

1 teaspoon extra-virgin olive oil

1 medium onion, thinly sliced

3 garlic cloves, minced

1 star anise pod

½ cup soy curls or sliced tofu

1 teaspoon freshly ground black pepper

3½ cups water

3 tablespoons soy sauce or tamari

4 ounces thin rice noodles, soaked in hot water for 10 minutes and drained

¼ cup roughly chopped fresh mint or basil leaves

¼ cup stemmed and chopped cilantro

1 jalapeño pepper, thinly sliced

2 scallions, thinly sliced

1 lime or lemon, halved

1. In a large saucepan over medium-high heat, add the oil and onion. Sauté, stirring, until the onion is golden, about 5 minutes. Add the garlic, anise, soy curls, and pepper. Sauté, stirring, for 2 minutes more.

2. Add the water and soy sauce, cover, and simmer for 15 minutes.

3. Remove the lid and using a spoon, remove and discard the anise pod.

4. Divide the noodles into two bowls and ladle the broth over, taking care to evenly distribute the soy curls or tofu.

5. Garnish each bowl with 2 tablespoons mint, 2 tablespoons cilantro, jalapeño, and scallions.

6. Squeeze lime or lemon over each bowl before serving.

PREP TIME:
5 MINUTES

COOK TIME:
25 MINUTES

Chipotle-Spiced Black Bean Soup

This hearty soup is great on its own, but lends itself well to add-ons, such as avocado, salsa, or crushed tortilla chips. For a full-throttle Mexican fiesta in a bowl, ladle it over rice, and serve with a heap of guacamole and a side of warm tortillas.

1. In a large saucepan over medium-high heat, add the oil, onion, garlic, red bell pepper, and cumin powder. Sauté, stirring, for 3 minutes. Add the chipotle peppers, beans, and water. Simmer for 20 minutes.

2. Using an immersion or standard blender, purée the soup, leaving some whole beans for texture.

3. Season with salt, and garnish with cilantro (if using) before serving.

TIP: *Chipotle peppers in adobo sauce are usually sold in small 7-ounce cans. For most recipes, you'll only need one or two peppers, but when transferred to a glass jar and refrigerated, they'll keep for a week or longer. Try adding a minced pepper to your next tofu scramble, or blending it into ketchup for a spicy dipping sauce.*

1 teaspoon extra-virgin olive oil

1 small onion, finely chopped

2 garlic cloves, minced

1 red bell pepper, seeded and chopped

1 teaspoon cumin powder

2 chipotle peppers in adobo sauce, minced

2 (15-ounce) cans black beans, drained and rinsed

3 cups water

Salt

¼ cup chopped fresh cilantro (optional)

West African Peanut Stew

In Mali, Senegal, and other West African countries, this stew is called *maafe* and is often served with rice. With or without a starchy side, this rich concoction tastes divine. If you like a little more fire in your bowl, add a splash of red hot sauce.

PREP TIME:
10 MINUTES

COOK TIME:
25 MINUTES

1 teaspoon extra-virgin olive oil

1 small onion, minced

1 jalapeño pepper, seeded and chopped

1-inch piece fresh ginger, finely chopped

½ teaspoon curry powder

1 large sweet potato, peeled and cubed

¼ cup peanut butter

1 (5-ounce) can coconut milk

1 large tomato, chopped

2½ cups water

Salt

Freshly ground black pepper

1. In a medium saucepan over medium-high heat, add the oil, onion, jalapeño, ginger, and curry powder. Sauté, stirring, for 3 minutes. Add the sweet potato and sauté for 2 minutes more.

2. In a small bowl or large measuring cup, stir together the peanut butter and coconut milk. Pour into the sweet potato mixture and stir.

3. Lower the heat. Add the tomato and water. Simmer, covered, for 20 minutes.

4. Season with salt and pepper. Serve hot.

TIP: *Peanut butter has come a long way since the ol' PB&J. When blended in equal measure with coconut milk and a dash of red chili sauce, it is transformed into an Indonesian-style satay marinade, a decadent dip for veggies, or a rich sauce for noodles.*

OUTRAGEOUS ONE-POT MEALS

Great Greek Phyllo Bake

PREP TIME:
15 MINUTES

COOK TIME:
30 MINUTES

Tofu, when seasoned with oregano and freshly squeezed lemon juice, takes on a feta-like flavor that marries perfectly with spinach. Lentils add protein and texture, and the crunchy phyllo topping makes digging into this one-pot dish feel like a special occasion.

1. Preheat the oven to 375°F.

2. In a medium nonstick skillet over medium heat, add 1 teaspoon oil, onion, garlic, and oregano. Sauté, stirring, for 4 minutes. Add the lentils and spinach. Cook for 3 minutes more, or until the spinach is wilted but still bright green. Season with ½ teaspoon salt and remove from the heat.

3. In a small bowl, add the crumbled tofu and lemon juice. Season with the remaining ½ teaspoon salt, add the olives, and stir to combine.

4. In a small baking pan, spoon in the lentil-spinach mixture. Spoon the tofu-olive mixture over the top. Place one sheet of phyllo pastry over the lentils-and-tofu mixture, and brush lightly with the remaining 2 teaspoons oil. Repeat with the remaining phyllo.

5. Bake for 20 minutes, or until the top layer is golden brown.

6. Serve hot or cold.

TIP: *Phyllo dough lasts forever—or several months, anyway— when properly sealed in a plastic bag and stored in the freezer. Using the thin sheets of dough is easy once you get the hang of it. Phyllo dough is good to have on hand for sweet and savory appetizers as well as also makeshift pie crusts.*

3 teaspoons extra-virgin olive oil, divided
1 small onion, finely chopped
1 garlic clove, minced
1 teaspoon dried oregano
1 cup cooked du Puy lentils
1 cup chopped spinach
1 teaspoon salt, divided
4 ounces tofu, crumbled
Juice of 1 lemon
10 black olives, roughly chopped
3 sheets phyllo pastry, trimmed to the size of your baking pan (should yield roughly six layers)

Cheesy Pasta Pie

Carbohydrates are the ultimate comfort food, and pasta is the queen of carbs. This lasagna-like pie gets its flavorsome goodness from a cheesy sauce and loads of vegetables, so it's healthy and comforting all at once. The breadcrumb topping adds crunch, and gives the pie an appealing golden hue. Cook the pasta ahead of time and allow it to cool before preparing.

PREP TIME:
10 MINUTES

COOK TIME:
30 MINUTES

For the pasta

1 teaspoon extra-virgin olive oil
1 small onion, peeled and chopped
1 teaspoon herbes de Provence
1 red bell pepper, seeded and cut into 1-inch-wide strips
1 zucchini, quartered lengthwise and cut into ½-inch slices
1 cup cremini mushrooms or other firm variety, thickly sliced
2 cups roughly chopped spinach
¼ cup red wine (optional)
2 cups rigatoni, penne, or ziti pasta, cooked until al dente and cooled

For the cheesy sauce

1 teaspoon cornstarch dissolved in 1 cup soy milk
½ cup nutritional yeast
2 tablespoons tomato paste
1 teaspoon salt
1 garlic clove, minced
Freshly ground black pepper
¼ cup breadcrumbs

To make the pasta

1. Preheat the oven to 450°F.

2. In a large nonstick skillet over medium-high heat, add the oil, onion, and herbes de Provence. Sauté for 3 minutes.

3. Add the bell pepper, zucchini, and mushrooms. Sauté, stirring, for 5 minutes.

4. Add the spinach and red wine (if using), and cook for 1 minute more. Remove from the heat, add the cooked pasta, and gently stir to combine.

To make the cheesy sauce

1. In a small saucepan over medium heat, add the cornstarch–soy milk mixture, nutritional yeast, tomato paste, salt, garlic, and pepper to taste. Bring to a simmer, stirring, until thickened, about 3 minutes.

2. In a lightly-oiled pie pan or small baking dish, spoon in the pasta-vegetable mixture. Pour the cheesy sauce over, top with the breadcrumbs, and bake for 15 minutes, or until golden.

'Shroomy Shepherd's Pie

Mushrooms in an herb-infused gravy are what give this classic potato-topped pie its meatiness and earthy flavor. Fast and easy to prepare, this dish is made even more simple when you make your mashed potatoes the day before.

1. Preheat the oven to 400°F.

2. In a medium saucepan over medium-high heat, add the potatoes and cover with the water. Simmer until tender, about 15 minutes. Drain and cool.

3. In a medium nonstick skillet over medium-high heat, add 1 teaspoon oil and the onion. Sauté for 3 minutes, then add the garlic, mushrooms, ½ teaspoon salt, and herbes de Provence. Sauté, stirring, for 5 minutes, then add the cornstarch-wine mixture. Bring to a simmer, and cook, stirring, for 2 minutes. Remove from the heat.

4. In a medium bowl, add the cooked potatoes, remaining 1 teaspoon oil, and remaining ½ teaspoon salt. Using a masher, mash the potatoes to desired consistency.

5. In a lightly oiled pie pan or small baking dish, add the mushroom mixture and pat down to cover the bottom of the pan. Add the corn, and spread to cover the mushroom mixture.

6. Top the pie off with a layer of mashed potatoes, and bake for 15 to 20 minutes, or until the potatoes are golden.

2 large potatoes, peeled and roughly chopped

3 cups water

2 teaspoons extra-virgin olive oil, divided

1 small onion, finely chopped

1 garlic clove, minced

2 cups roughly chopped mushrooms

1 teaspoon salt, divided

1 teaspoon herbes de Provence

1 teaspoon cornstarch, dissolved in ½ cup red wine

1 (8-ounce) can corn, drained (about 1 cup)

Creole Cornbread Bake

This hearty jambalaya-style dish is baked with a cornbread topping, making it a true all-in-one meal. If you're not a fan of okra, substitute zucchini instead, and you could easily swap out the soy curls for tofu or an equal measure of kidney beans for nearly identical results.

PREP TIME:
15 MINUTES

COOK TIME:
45 MINUTES

For the bake

- 1 small onion, diced
- 1 teaspoon extra-virgin olive oil
- 1 bell pepper, seeded and diced
- ½ cup soy curls, covered in hot water
- 2 garlic cloves, minced
- ½ teaspoon cayenne pepper
- ½ teaspoon smoked paprika
- 1 teaspoon salt
- ½ teaspoon freshly ground black pepper
- 2 large tomatoes, diced
- 1 cup fresh okra, sliced into ¼-inch pieces
- Corn kernels from 1 ear of corn, or about ½ cup
- ½ teaspoon cornstarch, blended with ½ cup cold water

For the cornbread topping

- ½ cup fine yellow cornmeal
- ½ cup all-purpose flour
- 1 teaspoon baking powder
- 1 teaspoon sugar
- ½ teaspoon salt
- 1 tablespoon extra-virgin olive oil, coconut oil, or vegan margarine
- 1 cup soy milk
- 2 teaspoons apple cider vinegar

To make the bake

1. Preheat the oven to 400°F.

2. In a medium-size nonstick skillet over medium-high heat, sauté the onion in oil for 3 minutes. Add the bell pepper and sauté 1 minute more.

3. Drain the soy curls and add them to the skillet along with the garlic, cayenne, paprika, salt, and pepper. Sauté, stirring, for 3 minutes.

4. Add the tomatoes, okra, and corn. Sauté for 2 minutes. Cover with the cornstarch-water mixture, lower the heat, and simmer for 5 minutes.

To make the cornbread topping

1. In a small mixing bowl, whisk together the cornmeal, flour, baking powder, sugar, and salt. Add the oil, soy milk, and vinegar. Whisk well to combine.

2. In a lightly oiled baking pan, add the tomato-okra mixture. Spoon the cornbread mixture on top, and bake for 30 minutes, or until golden.

3. Let cool slightly before serving.

TIP: *Don't have time for baking cornbread? Spoon the tomato-okra mixture over rice, sprinkle with cilantro or chopped parsley, and serve with a squeeze of lemon for an equally delectable and more time-thrifty meal.*

Italian Tofu Frittata

PREP TIME:
15 MINUTES

COOK TIME:
45 MINUTES

The chickpea flour in this recipe gives this baked frittata an egglike color and texture. For best results, let the flour and water mixture sit for an hour or two, or even overnight, to let the flavor to mellow. Hint: This tastes equally delicious served hot or at room temperature.

1. In a small bowl, combine the flour, water, and ½ teaspoon of salt. Stir to combine and let sit for 1 hour or longer.

2. Preheat the oven to 350°F.

3. In a food processor, add the tofu, nutritional yeast, remaining ½ teaspoon salt, and oregano. Season with pepper and blend until smooth.

4. Transfer the tofu mixture to a large bowl and stir in the olives, parsley, and spinach. Stir to combine, then pour in the chickpea flour mixture and gently stir to combine.

5. In a lightly oiled baking dish, spoon in the batter and bake for 45 minutes, or until golden.

6. Slice and serve with a heaping spoonful of Essential Marinara.

½ cup chickpea flour

1 cup water

1 teaspoon salt, divided

1 (8-ounce) package extra-firm tofu, rinsed and patted dry

2 tablespoons nutritional yeast

1 teaspoon oregano or herbes de Provence

Freshly ground black pepper

5 black olives, pitted and roughly chopped

½ cup finely chopped Italian parsley

1 cup roughly chopped spinach, chard, or kale

½ cup Essential Marinara (page 150) (optional)

Curried Quinoa-Cauliflower Bake

SOY-FREE

Rice is the grain that's most often associated with Indian cuisine, but here, quinoa steps in for an updated flavor pairing. Cauliflower and nuts add crunch, and raisins and coconut milk lend a subtle sweetness to this casserole that will entice you to double the recipe the next time.

PREP TIME:
15 MINUTES

COOK TIME:
45 MINUTES

1 cup quinoa, rinsed

2 cups water

1 teaspoon extra-virgin olive oil or coconut oil

2 teaspoons curry powder

1 onion, chopped

½ cauliflower head, cut into small florets (about 2½ cups)

2 large tomatoes, roughly chopped

1 teaspoon salt

1 large jalapeño or Anaheim chile, seeded and chopped

1 (5-ounce) can coconut milk

2 tablespoons raisins

¼ cup raw cashews

¼ cup chopped fresh cilantro

Lemon wedges, for garnish

1. Preheat the oven to 400°F.

2. In a medium saucepan over high heat, bring the quinoa and water to a boil. Reduce heat and simmer for 15 minutes, or until the quinoa has absorbed all the water. Remove from the heat and set aside.

3. In a large nonstick skillet over medium-high heat, add the oil, curry powder, and onion. Sauté, stirring, for 3 minutes. Add the cauliflower florets and cook for 3 minutes more.

4. Add the chopped tomatoes, salt, jalapeño, coconut milk, and raisins. Stir to combine, and remove from the heat. Add the quinoa, and stir gently to combine.

5. In a lightly oiled baking dish, pour the quinoa-cauliflower mixture. Sprinkle the cashews over the top, and bake for 20 minutes, or until the nuts are golden.

6. To serve, plate, and top with fresh cilantro and a squeeze of lemon.

PREP TIME:
10 MINUTES

COOK TIME:
20 MINUTES

Pea and Pimento Paella

Paella is a quintessentially Spanish one-pot meal that gets its special flavor from saffron and visual appeal from a colorful mélange of vegetables. This recipe lends itself to whatever vegetables are in season—green beans or asparagus, for example—and tastes great the next day.

1. In a large nonstick skillet or wok, add the oil and onion and sauté 3 minutes. Add the red bell pepper, zucchini, and paprika. Sauté for 5 minutes more, stirring.

2. Add the tomato paste, saffron, lemon juice, water, and salt. Bring to a simmer, then add the peas, rice, olives, and artichoke hearts. Stir to combine, and let cook for 3 minutes more, or until the water is absorbed.

3. To serve, garnish with a generous sprinkling of Italian parsley.

2 teaspoons extra-virgin olive oil
1 small onion, minced
1 small red bell pepper, cut into thin strips
1 small zucchini, cut lengthwise and thinly sliced
1 teaspoon smoked paprika
2 tablespoons tomato paste
Pinch saffron (about 5 strands)
Juice of ½ lemon
¼ cup water
1 teaspoon salt
½ cup fresh or frozen peas
1½ cups cooked white rice
10 black or green olives, pitted
4 frozen, canned, or jarred artichoke hearts, halved
¼ cup chopped Italian parsley

Deconstructed Burrito Bake

NUT-FREE
SOY-FREE

This is probably the easiest—and tastiest—one-pot meal you'll ever make. Don't fear the cans: Both beans and enchilada sauce are time-consuming to prepare from scratch, so the packaged varieties offer flavor and convenience. Shop your local natural food store for organic varieties.

PREP TIME:
10 MINUTES

COOK TIME:
30 MINUTES

1½ cups cooked brown or white rice

1 (15-ounce) can black beans or pinto beans, drained and rinsed

1 flour tortilla (or 2 corn tortillas), cut into thin strips

5 black olives, pitted and thinly sliced

1 (10-ounce) can green or red enchilada sauce

1 scallion, thinly sliced

1 tomato, roughly chopped

1 avocado, halved and seeded

Lime wedges

1. Preheat the oven to 400°F.

2. In a lightly oiled baking dish, add the brown rice, pressing to evenly cover the bottom of the pan. Add the beans, and spread to cover the rice. Top with the tortilla strips and olives, then smother in the enchilada sauce.

3. Bake for 30 minutes, or until bubbly and slightly browned on top.

4. To serve, garnish each serving with a sprinkling of scallion, half the tomato, half the avocado, and squeeze with fresh lime juice.

TIP: *Both corn and flour tortillas will last a month or more in the freezer if properly sealed. To revive your tortillas so they're ready to become a taco or burrito, simply pop them in a 300°F oven for 10 minutes.*

Savory Bread Pudding

PREP TIME:
10 MINUTES

COOK TIME:
30 MINUTES

Though sweet versions of this dish have been popular for years, the savory side of bread pudding is just catching on. Hearty and satisfying, this recipe is the ideal use for slightly stale bread, and adapts easily to match whatever spices and vegetables you have on hand. Try it the first time as written, and then make your own rules!

1. Preheat the oven to 400°F.

2. In a large nonstick skillet over medium-high heat, add the oil and onion. Sauté, stirring, for 3 minutes. Add the garlic, herbes de Provence, and kale. Cook, stirring, for 5 minutes more. Stir in the bread cubes, and cook for an additional 3 minutes. Remove from the heat.

3. In a small saucepan over medium heat, add the cornstarch–soy milk mixture, salt, mustard, nutritional yeast, and nutmeg. Simmer, stirring, for 4 minutes.

4. Remove from the heat.

5. In a lightly oiled baking pan, spoon in the bread mixture and pour the sauce over.

6. Bake for 20 minutes, or until the bread is golden brown, and dust with pepper before serving.

1½ tablespoons extra-virgin olive oil

1 small onion, minced

1 garlic clove, minced

1 teaspoon herbes de Provence

3 cups stemmed and roughly chopped kale

½ baguette, thickly sliced and cut into cubes (about 2 cups)

1 teaspoon cornstarch, dissolved in 1 cup soy milk

½ teaspoon salt

1 teaspoon Dijon mustard

¼ cup nutritional yeast

⅛ teaspoon grated nutmeg

Freshly ground black pepper

Bibimbap Bowl

The secret to the popular Korean dish Bibimbap is the sweet-hot chili sauce, which you add in generous dollops and stir into your bowl. If buying commercial kimchi to accompany your meal, check the ingredients list twice to ensure there's not fish hiding inside. Cooking the rice beforehand shaves time off the prep process.

PREP TIME:
15 MINUTES

COOK TIME:
25 MINUTES

For the Korean barbecue sauce

3 tablespoons red chili sauce with garlic

1 tablespoon agave nectar or maple syrup

1 tablespoon hoisin sauce

1 teaspoon soy sauce or wheat-free tamari

For the Bibimbap

3 teaspoons sesame oil, divided

6 shiitake mushrooms, thickly sliced

2 teaspoons soy sauce or wheat-free tamari, divided

1 garlic clove, minced

½ (8-ounce) container firm tofu, rinsed, patted dry, and sliced into thick matchsticks

1 carrot, cut into matchsticks

3 cups roughly chopped spinach

2 tablespoons water

2 cups cooked rice

1 scallion, thinly sliced

To make the Korean barbecue sauce

In a small bowl, combine the red chili sauce, agave or maple syrup, hoisin sauce, and soy sauce, and stir to combine.

To make the Bibimbap

1. In a medium nonstick skillet over medium-high heat, add 1 teaspoon sesame oil and cook the shiitake mushrooms, stirring, for 3 minutes. Season with 1 teaspoon soy sauce and stir. Remove the mushrooms immediately and set aside.

2. Return the skillet to the stove and add 1 teaspoon sesame oil followed by the garlic, tofu, and carrots. Sauté, stirring, for 5 minutes. Remove the tofu and carrots and set aside.

3. Return the skillet to the stove. Add the spinach and remaining 1 teaspoon soy sauce, remaining 1 teaspoon sesame oil, and 2 tablespoons water. Lower the heat, cover, and steam for 3 minutes, or until the spinach is wilted but still bright green.

4. To serve, scoop 1 cup of rice into each bowl. Over the top, arrange half the mushrooms, half the carrot-tofu mixture, and half the spinach.

5. Sprinkle with scallions, and season with the Korean barbecue sauce.

TIP: *Cover your uncooked, unseasoned leftover tofu with cold water and store, refrigerated, in a sealed container for up to four days, changing the water daily to keep the tofu fresh.*

PREP TIME:
10 MINUTES

COOK TIME:
10 MINUTES

Chickpea Paella

Paella is a quintessentially Spanish one-pot meal that gets its special flavor from saffron and visual appeal from a colorful mélange of vegetables. This recipe lends itself to whatever vegetables are in season—green beans or asparagus, for example—and tastes great the next day.

1. In a large non-stick skillet or wok, add the olive oil and onion and sauté 3 minutes. Add the green beans, red bell pepper, and smoked paprika and sauté for 5 minutes more, stirring.

2. Add the tomato paste, saffron, lemon juice, water, and salt. Bring to a simmer, then add the chickpeas and rice. Stir to combine, and let cook for 3 minutes more, or until the water is absorbed. To serve, garnish with a generous sprinkling of Italian parsley.

2 teaspoons olive oil

1 small onion, minced

2 cups green beans, washed, trimmed, and sliced in half lengthwise

1 small red bell pepper, washed and sliced into thin strips

1 teaspoon smoked paprika

2 tablespoons tomato paste

1 pinch saffron (about 5 strands)

1 tablespoon lemon juice

¼ cup water

Salt

1 (15-ounce) can chickpeas, rinsed and drained

1½ cups cooked white rice

¼ cup Italian parsley, chopped

Easiest Curry Bowls

Though it might not completely replace your favorite Thai take-out, this warming pot of noodles, tofu, vegetables, and just enough spice is sure to become a second staple. Do keep in mind that many pre-packaged curry pastes contain non-vegan ingredients, so be sure to read your labels carefully.

PREP TIME:
10 MINUTES

COOK TIME:
20 MINUTES

1 tablespoon vegetable oil
½ yellow onion, thinly sliced
1 carrot, thinly sliced
1½ teaspoons red curry paste
1 teaspoon freshly grated ginger
2 cups vegetable broth
1 cup coconut milk
½ cup broccoli florets
1 cup firm tofu, cubed (about ½ of a 14-ounce package)
4 ounces rice noodles
2 teaspoons chopped scallions

1. In a medium saucepan over medium heat, add the oil, onion, carrot, curry paste, and ginger. Sauté, stirring, for 5 minutes, until the onions begin to brown and the carrot softens slightly.

2. Add the vegetable broth and coconut milk, and bring to a simmer.

3. Add the broccoli and tofu, and simmer for 3 minutes.

4. Add the rice noodles, simmer for 4 minutes, then remove from heat.

5. Serve garnished with scallions.

TOSS IT TOGETHER TIP: *If you have leftover scallions, make an herbaceous salad dressing by blending them with olive oil, seasoned rice vinegar, and a little bit of Dijon mustard.*

PERFECT PIZZAS & PASTAS

PREP TIME:
10 MINUTES

COOK TIME:
20 MINUTES

Meaty Mushroom Stroganoff

Stroganoff has Russian origins and is typically made with non-vegan ingredients, but the heart and soul of this recipe are the creamy noodles, which are simple to prepare using plant-based alternatives. Here, non-dairy yogurt and fettucini noodles do the job perfectly. Cook the pasta ahead of time.

1. In a large nonstick skillet over medium heat, add oil the and onion. Sauté for 3 minutes. Add the garlic and paprika and sauté 2 minutes more.

2. Add the mushrooms and cook, stirring, for 5 minutes. Pour in the red wine, and let simmer for 3 minutes.

3. Add the non-dairy yogurt and fettucini. Stir to combine.

4. To serve, season with salt and pepper. Sprinkle with the parsley.

TIP: *The stroganoff mixture isn't just a tasty topping for noodles; it can also be spooned over baked potatoes, cooked rice, or even toast!*

1 teaspoon extra-virgin
   olive oil
1 small onion, thinly sliced
1 garlic clove, minced
½ teaspoon smoked paprika
2 cups thinly sliced cremini,
   Portobello, or other firm
   mushrooms
¼ cup red wine
¼ cup non-dairy yogurt
Cooked fettucini for 2 people
Salt
Freshly ground black pepper
¼ cup chopped Italian parsley

Penne with Garlic Crème

Flavor and comfort collide in this rich and garlicky pasta dish. The creaminess comes from an unexpected source—beans—providing a good wallop of protein and fiber with every serving. A fresh salad is the ideal accompaniment to this dish, and a glass of wine is also highly recommended. Cook the pasta ahead of time.

2 teaspoons extra-virgin olive oil

3 garlic cloves, minced

1 (15-ounce) can white beans, rinsed and drained

1 cup non-dairy milk

1 teaspoon salt

Cooked penne noodles for 2 people

Freshly ground black pepper

Pinch red pepper flakes (optional)

1. In a large nonstick skillet over medium heat, add the oil and garlic. Cook for 3 minutes. Add the beans and sauté, stirring, for 2 minutes.

2. Using an immersion or standard blender, purée the bean-garlic mixture, non-dairy milk, and salt together until smooth. Return the sauce to the pan and simmer for 2 minutes.

3. Add the penne to the pot, stir to coat, and remove from the heat.

4. Serve with pepper and red pepper flakes (if using).

PREP TIME:
15 MINUTES

Raw Zucchini Primavera

Raw pasta is easy to make at home with one utensil you likely have in your culinary arsenal already: a potato peeler. Fresh but filling, this pasta makes a great on-the-go warm-weather meal. The recipe calls for zucchini, but you could also use yellow summer squash.

1. In a medium bowl, combine the tomatoes, garlic, salt, and oil (if using). Using an immersion or standard blender, purée until smooth.

2. Add the zucchini ribbons to the tomato-garlic sauce.

3. Add the olives and scallions. Toss to combine.

TIP: *There are a number of contraptions on the market designed to make prepping vegetable noodles at home that much easier. Look for products marketed as "spiralizers," many of which also work as mandolines for slicing other vegetables, such as potatoes for homemade fries.*

2 large tomatoes
2 garlic cloves, halved
½ teaspoon salt
1 teaspoon extra-virgin olive oil (optional)
2 medium zucchini, sliced into thin ribbons with a potato peeler
5 black olives, roughly chopped
1 scallion, thinly sliced

Pumpkin-Sage Farfalle

NUT-FREE
SOY-FREE

PREP TIME:
10 MINUTES

COOK TIME:
30 MINUTES

While this recipe calls for farfalle—otherwise known as bowtie noodles—
you could use any pasta you fancy, from spaghetti to fusilli. For added flavor,
add a generous dusting of nutritional yeast, which imparts a cheese-like flavor.
Cook the pasta ahead of time.

1 small pumpkin, butternut, or
   other firm squash, peeled
   and cut into cubes

1 small onion,
   roughly chopped

3 garlic cloves, quartered

1 tablespoon fresh sage,
   or 2 teaspoons dried

2 tablespoons extra-virgin
   olive oil, divided

1 teaspoon salt

Cooked farfalle noodles for
   2 people

Freshly ground black pepper

1. Preheat the oven to 400°F.

2. In a large bowl, add the squash, onion, garlic, and sage. Drizzle
with 1½ tablespoons oil and stir to combine. Pour the mixture onto a
baking sheet, season with the salt, and bake for 30 minutes.

3. In a large bowl, add the cooked noodles and remaining ½ tablespoon
oil. Remove the squash mixture from the oven and toss in with the
noodles, stirring to combine.

4. Season with pepper. Serve immediately.

PREP TIME:
5 MINUTES

COOK TIME:
25 MINUTES

Pasta e Fagioli

This soupy pasta-and-beans dish is an old Italian peasant food that's nourishing and hearty, and traditionally vegetarian. Try it with different, seasonal beans, such as fava or borlotti, and experiment with different sizes and shapes of pasta to add visual appeal to the meal. Cook the pasta ahead of time.

1. In a large saucepan over medium-high heat, add the oil, carrot, and onion. Sauté for 3 minutes. Add the garlic and herbes de Provence. Sauté for 3 minutes more.

2. Add the tomato purée, wine, water, and salt. Simmer, stirring, for 10 minutes. Add the beans, noodles, and greens and stir to combine. Let simmer for 5 minutes more.

3. Season with pepper and serve with crusty Italian bread.

2 teaspoons extra-virgin olive oil

1 carrot, finely chopped

1 small onion, finely chopped

2 garlic cloves, minced

1 teaspoon herbes de Provence

1 (15-ounce) can tomato purée

¼ cup red wine

¼ cup water

1 teaspoon salt

1 (15-ounce) can cannellini beans, rinsed and drained

Cooked tubetti, macaroni, or other small noodles for 2 people

2 cups chopped spinach, kale, or chard

Freshly ground black pepper

Italian bread, for serving

Pasta Bolognese with Lentils

Once you've cooked the noodles and the lentils, this savory supper comes together in no time flat. The lentils add a meaty texture and the grated vegetables add color and nutrients. To kick up the flavor another notch, add crushed garlic and a pinch of red pepper flakes.

PREP TIME:
5 MINUTES

COOK TIME:
10 MINUTES

1 teaspoon extra-virgin olive oil

1 small zucchini, grated

1 small carrot, grated

½ cup cooked du Puy Lentils

1 cup Essential Marinara (page 150)

Cooked noodles of choice for 2 people

Salt

Freshly ground black pepper

1. In a medium saucepan over medium heat, add the oil, zucchini, and carrot. Sauté for 3 minutes. Add the lentils and Essential Marinara. Simmer, stirring, for 3 minutes.

2. To serve, plate the pasta and spoon the warm sauce over. Season with salt and pepper.

PREP TIME:
10 MINUTES

COOK TIME:
10 MINUTES

Puttanesca Verde

Verde is Italian for "green," and this pasta dish is loaded with the color of spring. For an even brighter dose of green on your plate, use a pasta made with spinach, or serve the sauce over homemade zucchini noodles for a lighter take. Cook the pasta ahead of time.

1. In a large nonstick skillet over medium-high heat, add the oil, capers, and garlic. Sauté, stirring, for 3 minutes, then add the olives, scallions, and red pepper flakes (if using). Cook, stirring, for 3 minutes more.

2. Add the spinach and sauté for 1 minute, or until the spinach is soft but still bright green.

3. Add the spaghetti and toss to combine. Just before serving, stir in the basil and season with salt.

1 tablespoon extra-virgin olive oil

1 tablespoon capers, rinsed

3 garlic cloves, minced

½ cup pitted green olives, roughly chopped

2 scallions, thinly sliced

Pinch red pepper flakes (optional)

2 cups roughly chopped spinach

Cooked spaghetti for 2 people

¼ cup roughly chopped fresh basil

½ teaspoon salt

Creamy Truffled Linguini

Truffle oil is usually made with a synthetic truffle flavor that tastes, more or less, identical to the real thing, yet costs a fraction of what fresh truffles fetch. The trick to this recipe is to add the oil at the very end, to finish the dish, rather than cooking with it.

PREP TIME:
10 MINUTES

COOK TIME:
15 MINUTES

1 teaspoon extra-virgin olive oil

1 small onion, finely chopped

1 garlic clove, minced

2 cups roughly chopped mushrooms

2 teaspoons cornstarch, dissolved in 1 cup non-dairy milk

2 tablespoons nutritional yeast

1 teaspoon salt

Cooked linguini for 2 people

Freshly ground black pepper

1 teaspoon truffle oil

1. In a medium nonstick skillet over medium heat, add the oil and onion. Cook, stirring, for 3 minutes. Add the garlic and cook 2 minutes more.

2. Add the mushrooms and sauté, stirring, for 5 minutes.

3. Add the cornstarch-milk mixture, nutritional yeast, and salt. Simmer, stirring, until thick and bubbly, about 4 minutes.

4. Stir in the linguini and season with pepper.

5. To serve, plate and drizzle each serving with ½ teaspoon of the truffle oil.

PREP TIME:
10 MINUTES

COOK TIME:
5 MINUTES

Sesame-Peanut Noodles

Peanuts give this dish crunch and a fatty richness, but if you or your dining companion have an allergy, use toasted walnuts or pine nuts instead. The key ingredient holding this dish together is the sesame oil, which will last for months and months if stored in the refrigerator.

1. In a medium saucepan over medium heat, add the sesame oil, garlic, ginger, and scallions. Sauté, stirring, for 2 minutes.

2. And the spinach and sauté for 2 minutes more.

3. Add the spaghetti and toss to combine, then pour in the sugar-soy sauce mixture. Just before serving, stir in the chopped peanuts.

2 teaspoons sesame oil

1 garlic clove

½-inch piece fresh ginger, peeled and minced

2 scallions, thinly sliced

1 cup roughly chopped spinach or bok choy

Cooked spaghetti for 2 people

1 teaspoon sugar, agave, or maple syrup, dissolved in 2 tablespoons soy sauce or tamari

2 tablespoons chopped peanuts

Pad Thai with Tofu

The cilantro and the slightly sweet sauce give this Pad Thai its Southeast Asian flavor. For an even more authentic taste, add ½ teaspoon minced lemongrass to the tofu as it cooks. You'll find it in the freezer section of Asian markets, where it is usually sold in little plastic jars or larger bags.

PREP TIME:
15 MINUTES

COOK TIME:
10 MINUTES

1 teaspoon peanut, coconut, or canola oil

½ (8-ounce) package tofu, drained, patted dry, and chopped into cubes

¼ cup peanut butter, mixed with ¼ cup water

1 teaspoon red chili sauce

Juice of 1 lime

1 teaspoon sugar, agave, or maple syrup, dissolved in 2 tablespoons soy sauce or tamari

Cooked rice noodles for 2 people

¼ cup chopped fresh cilantro

1 scallion, chopped

Lemon or lime wedges, for garnish

1. In a large saucepan over medium-high heat, add the oil and tofu and sauté, stirring, for 5 minutes. Lower the heat and stir in the peanut butter–water mixture, chili sauce, lime juice, and sugar–soy sauce mixture. Add the rice noodles and cilantro. Stir to combine.

2. To serve, garnish with the scallion and a squeeze of lemon or lime juice.

TIP: *Rice noodles can be extra sticky once they're cooled, but if you drizzle the drained noodles with a bit of oil, it will make the serving process easier. Bland oils, such as canola or peanut oil, are the best bets for the job.*

PREP TIME:
10 MINUTES

COOK TIME:
20 MINUTES

Green Chile Mac 'n' Cheese

This stovetop mac 'n' cheese could also be topped with breadcrumbs and baked for 20 minutes for a less saucy, more crunchy version. To make this dish gluten-free, substitute quinoa or another noodle variety for the standard-issue macaroni.

1. In a large nonstick skillet over medium heat, add the oil and onion. Sauté for 3 minutes. Add the garlic and cumin and sauté 2 minutes more.

2. Add the cornstarch-milk mixture, nutritional yeast, and salt. Simmer, stirring, for 4 minutes.

3. Add the chiles and noodles. Stir.

4. Serve immediately.

1 teaspoon extra-virgin olive oil

1 small onion, chopped

1 garlic clove, minced

½ teaspoon ground cumin

2 teaspoons cornstarch, dissolved in 1 cup non-dairy milk

¼ cup nutritional yeast

1 teaspoon salt

1 (4-ounce) can chopped green chiles

Cooked macaroni for 2 people

Sicilian Fusilli with Olives and Raisins

This recipe couldn't be simpler to make, or more delicious. The sweetness of raisins provides a really enjoyable contrast to the saltiness of the green olives. Serve this with a glass of your favorite red table wine for the full Sicilian experience.

PREP TIME:
10 MINUTES

COOK TIME:
15 MINUTES

2 teaspoons extra-virgin
   olive oil
1 small onion, thinly sliced
2 garlic cloves, thinly sliced
1 small eggplant, cubed
   (about 2½ cups)
1 teaspoon herbes de Provence
3 tablespoons tomato paste
1 cup water
¼ cup raisins
¼ cup red or green olives,
   pitted and chopped
Cooked fusilli for 2 people
1 teaspoon salt
¼ cup roughly chopped
   Italian parsley

1. In a large nonstick skillet over medium-high heat, add the oil, onion, garlic, eggplant, and herbes de Provence. Sauté for 5 minutes.

2. Add the tomato paste, water, raisins, and olives. Stir to combine.

3. Cover, lower the heat, and simmer for 10 minutes.

4. To serve, spoon over the fusilli, season with the salt, and sprinkle with parsley.

PREP TIME:
10 MINUTES

COOK TIME:
10 MINUTES

Tomato-Caper Pasta

Sometimes, the simplest recipes yield the most delicious and memorable results. This dish is one of those, relying on just a handful of ingredients to bring oodles of flavor to the plate. If you can't find cherry tomatoes at your local grocery, use whatever you've got on hand, but don't skimp on the basil!

1. In a medium nonstick skillet over medium-high heat, add the oil and garlic. Sauté for 2 minutes. Add the cherry tomatoes, capers, and vinegar. Stir.

2. Reduce the heat, cover, and simmer for 5 minutes.

3. To serve, add the cooked spaghetti and basil to the pan. Stir to combine. Season with salt and pepper.

2 teaspoons extra-virgin olive oil

3 garlic cloves, minced

2 cups cherry tomatoes, sliced in half

1 tablespoon roughly chopped capers

1 tablespoon red wine vinegar

Cooked spaghetti for 2 people

¼ cup finely chopped fresh basil

Salt

Freshly ground black pepper

Sweet Potato Gnocchi with Sage

NUT-FREE
SOY-FREE
QUICK & EASY

This simple recipe takes the mystery out of the gnocchi-making process. The dough is a straightforward blend of potato, flour, salt, and oil that takes minutes to throw together. The results taste like you labored for hours.

PREP TIME:
10 MINUTES

COOK TIME:
15 MINUTES

1 large sweet potato, baked and cooled, skin removed (about ¾ cup)

½ teaspoon salt

¾ cup all-purpose flour

1 tablespoon extra-virgin olive oil, plus 1 teaspoon, divided

¼ cup chopped fresh sage leaves

1 garlic clove, minced

1. Bring a large pot of salted water to a boil, then reduce to a simmer.

2. In a medium bowl, combine the sweet potato, salt, flour, and 1 teaspoon oil. Stir gently to combine.

3. On a floured work surface, knead the sweet potato dough for 30 seconds, then roll into a cylindrical shape. Slice into ½-inch-long sections, and gently press each gnocchi piece with a fork on each side.

4. Gently slide the gnocchi into the simmering water. They will immediately sink to the bottom. Cover, and cook for 3 minutes, then remove the lid. The gnocchi will be floating on top now. Simmer, cooking, for 2 to 3 minutes more, then gently drain and rinse with cold water to halt the cooking process.

5. In a large nonstick skillet over medium heat, add the remaining 1 tablespoon oil, sage, and garlic. Cook, stirring, for 2 minutes.

6. Add the gnocchi and sauté for 1 minute, or until the gnocchi is warmed through and coated with sage oil. Serve immediately.

Orzo with Walnuts and Peas

PREP TIME:
10 MINUTES

COOK TIME:
10 MINUTES

One of the tiniest and most versatile pastas is orzo, which is shaped like rice and can be used almost interchangeably as rice or pasta. Here, it's paired with peas and walnuts, which are added at the end to give the dish a rich crunchiness. Cook the pasta ahead of time.

1. In a medium nonstick skillet over medium-high heat, add the oil and onion. Sauté for 3 minutes.

2. Add the garlic and cook for 2 minutes more.

3. Add the orzo to the pan and stir, followed by the peas, milk, and salt, and season with pepper.

4. Cook, stirring, for 3 minutes, or until the peas are done and the milk has evaporated.

5. Just before serving, stir in the walnuts and Italian parsley.

1 teaspoon extra-virgin olive oil

1 small onion, minced

1 garlic clove, minced

1½ cups cooked orzo pasta

¼ cup frozen peas

¼ cup non-dairy milk

1 teaspoon salt

Freshly ground black pepper

¼ cup toasted walnut pieces

¼ cup finely chopped Italian parsley

Smoky Red Pepper Pasta

SOY-FREE
QUICK & EASY

PREP TIME:
10 MINUTES

COOK TIME:
10 MINUTES

Here's a little secret: You can use yellow or even orange peppers for this sweet-and-savory pasta. The smoked paprika will lend a deeper red color to the sauce, and no one will know the difference.

2 large red bell peppers, roasted, peeled, seeded, and cut into chunks

2 garlic cloves, minced

1 teaspoon smoked paprika

2 teaspoons extra-virgin olive oil

½ teaspoon salt

Cooked rigatoni for 2 people

1 scallion, thinly sliced

Almond Parmesan (page 155) (optional)

1. In a food processor, pulse the red peppers with the garlic, paprika, oil, and salt.

2. In a medium saucepan over medium heat, add the red pepper mixture and simmer for 5 minutes.

3. Add the pasta and stir to coat.

4. To serve, sprinkle with the scallion and dust with Almond Parmesan (if using).

TIP: *A vegan shortcut to this recipe would be to top the rigatoni with bottled Ajvar, an Eastern European dip and spread that's available in most well-stocked supermarkets and natural-food stores. It has a slightly sweeter flavor and a beautiful, orange-red hue.*

Sensational Stuffed Shells

PREP TIME:
10 MINUTES

COOK TIME:
30 MINUTES

These shells are stuffed with a savory tofu-herb mixture and baked. If you're pressed for time, simply warm the sauce up on the stovetop and spoon over the shells immediately after filling them with the ricotta-style tofu.

1. Preheat the oven to 400°F.

2. In a large bowl, crumble the tofu into small pieces. Add the oregano, salt, and nutritional yeast.

3. In a medium nonstick skillet over medium-high heat, add the oil and garlic. Sauté for 2 minutes. Add the spinach and sauté for 2 minutes, or until the spinach is wilted and the liquid has evaporated.

4. Spoon the spinach-garlic mixture into the tofu and add the lemon juice. Stir to combine, then stuff each shell generously with the mixture.

5. In a small baking dish, spoon in 3 tablespoons of Essential Marinara and spread to cover the bottom. Gently place the stuffed shells on top, then spoon the remaining sauce over the top. Cover with foil and bake for 15 minutes, then remove and bake 10 minutes more.

6. To serve, add a dollop of Cashew Crème.

TIP: *If you like a saucier shell, leave them face up when baking. If you like a drier texture, stuff them with a bit less filling and place them seam down in the pan before topping with sauce and popping them in the oven.*

½ (8-ounce) package firm tofu, rinsed and squeezed dry between two tea towels

1 teaspoon dried oregano

½ teaspoon salt

1 tablespoon nutritional yeast

1 teaspoon extra-virgin olive oil

2 garlic cloves, minced

3 cups roughly chopped fresh spinach

Juice of ½ lemon

Cooked jumbo pasta shells for 2 people, or about 8 shells

1 cup of Essential Marinara (page 150)

Cashew Crème (page 153) (optional)

Pesto-Olive Pie

NUT-FREE
SOY-FREE

Homemade spinach pesto gives this pizza a healthy dose of garlic-infused flavor with every slice. Just realized you're out of the green stuff? Substitute Essential Marinara (page 150) for a more traditional and equally tasty red-sauce pie, and top with an extra clove of crushed garlic for extra potency.

PREP TIME:
10 MINUTES

COOK TIME:
30 MINUTES

1 20-Minute Pizza Dough
   (page 152)
3 tablespoons Spinach Pesto
   (page 151)
1 zucchini, thinly sliced
10 olives, thinly sliced
Extra-virgin olive oil,
   for drizzling
Salt
Freshly ground black pepper
Red pepper flakes
Almond Parmesan (page 155)

1. Preheat the oven to 425°F.

2. Roll the 20-Minute Pizza Dough out onto a lightly oiled pizza pan.

3. Spread the pesto evenly over the dough.

4. Arrange the zucchini slices over the pesto, followed by the olives. Drizzle with oil and season with salt and pepper.

5. Bake on the top rack of the oven for 30 minutes.

6. To serve, dust with red pepper flakes and sprinkle with Almond Parmesan.

TIP: *If you don't feel like dividing your pie into two halves, transform the dough into smaller mini pizzas instead. This way, you'll have more creative freedom to experiment with sauces and toppings. The dough will also keep overnight in the refrigerator if coated with a bit of extra-virgin olive oil and wrapped in plastic.*

Curried Potato Pizza

PREP TIME:
10 MINUTES

COOK TIME:
30 MINUTES

Take your favorite Indian dish, replace the rice with a pizza crust, and you've got a surprisingly tasty twist on the usual Italian-style pizza. Play with the toppings—cauliflower florets or cooked chickpeas would make interesting additions—and crank up the heat with sliced jalapeño peppers, if you like a bit of fire.

1. Preheat the oven to 425°F.

2. Roll the 20-Minute Pizza Dough out onto a lightly oiled pizza pan.

3. In a small bowl, combine the Cashew Crème and curry powder. Spread the mixture evenly over dough.

4. Arrange the potato slices over the Cashew Crème, followed by the onion slices and olives. Drizzle with oil and season with salt and red pepper flakes.

5. Bake on the top rack of the oven for 30 minutes.

6. To serve, sprinkle with the cilantro (if using) and a squeeze of lemon.

1 20-Minute Pizza Dough (page 152)

3 tablespoons Cashew Crème (page 153)

1 teaspoon curry powder

1 large potato, peeled, thinly sliced, and steamed until tender

1 small onion, thinly sliced

10 olives, thinly sliced

Extra-virgin olive oil for drizzling

Salt

Red pepper flakes

1/3 cup fresh cilantro leaves (optional)

Lemon wedges

Creamy Artichoke Pizza

SOY-FREE

In Italy, you'll always find artichoke pizza on the menu, and more often than not, it's inherently vegan. To make it at home, you'll need artichoke hearts, garlic, and plenty of willpower. Why? This pie smells irresistible when it bakes, but it's definitely worth the wait.

PREP TIME:
10 MINUTES

COOK TIME:
30 MINUTES

1 20-Minute Pizza Dough
   (page 152)
2 cups frozen, canned, or
   jarred artichoke hearts
3 tablespoons Cashew Crème
   (page 153), thinned with
   ¼ cup non-dairy milk
4 garlic cloves, minced
1 teaspoon oregano
1 teaspoon salt
Freshly ground black pepper
Red pepper flakes
Almond Parmesan (page 155)

1. Preheat oven to 425°F.

2. Roll the 20-Minute Pizza Dough out onto a lightly oiled pizza pan.

3. In a food processor, combine the artichoke hearts, Cashew Crème, garlic, oregano, and salt. Pulse until almost smooth, leaving a few chunks.

4. Spread mixture over the dough and bake for 30 minutes. To serve, dust with the black pepper and red pepper flakes and sprinkle with Almond Parmesan.

PREP TIME:
10 MINUTES

COOK TIME:
10 MINUTES

Pasta with Vegetables

The flavors of the Italian Mediterranean dominate this simple, rustic pasta dish that gets an unexpected crunch from toasted almonds. If you can't find egg-free tagliatelle noodles, use linguini or farfalle instead for equally tasty results.

1. Cook the pasta until al dente, then rinse and set aside.

2. Meanwhile, in a medium-size saucepan over medium heat, add 1 tablespoon olive oil and the garlic. Let cook for 1 minute, stirring. Add the artichoke hearts and olives, and cook for 2 minutes more.

3. Add the pasta to the pan, and add the remaining 1 tablespoon olive oil. Stir to coat the pasta with the olive oil–artichoke mixture, then add the lemon juice and toss. Remove from the heat.

4. To serve, top each serving with the toasted almonds and Italian parsley, and season with salt and freshly ground black pepper to taste.

Tagliatelle for 2 people

2 tablespoons olive oil, divided

1 garlic clove, thinly sliced

1 (15-ounce) can artichoke hearts, rinsed, drained, and roughly chopped

1 cup green olives, rinsed, pitted, and sliced in half lengthwise

1 tablespoon lemon juice

½ cup toasted almonds

2 tablespoons Italian parsley, roughly chopped

Salt

Freshly ground black pepper

Summertime Zesty Pizza

SOY-FREE

This pie really shines at the peak of tomato season, when you can almost taste the sunshine in every bite. Heirloom tomatoes tend to have a more delicate flavor than other varieties, and they pair beautifully with the fresh pop of lemon zest.

PREP TIME:
10 MINUTES

COOK TIME:
30 MINUTES

1 20-Minute Pizza Dough
(page 152)

3 tablespoons Cashew Crème
(page 153)

Zest of 1 lemon

1 large heirloom tomato,
thinly sliced

¼ cup fresh basil, thinly sliced

1. Preheat oven to 425°F.

2. Roll out the 20-Minute Pizza Dough onto a lightly oiled pizza pan.

3. Spread the Cashew Crème over the pizza, then sprinkle the zest evenly over the top.

4. Lay the tomato slices in a single layer over the pizza.

5. Bake on the top rack in the oven for 30 minutes.

6. Remove from the oven, top with the basil, and serve.

CHAPTER

8

DECADENT DESSERTS

Nutty Fudge

PREP TIME:
5 MINUTES

COOK TIME:
5 MINUTES

Finding the perfect small-size cookware for two can sometimes pose a challenge. For this fudge, try using an ice-cube tray or a muffin pan as a mold. You'll get nicely portioned morsels that are perfect for two and a readymade storage container for any extras.

1. In a small bowl over a pot of simmering water, add the margarine, sugar, salt, cocoa powder, vanilla, and milk. Stir until smooth and well-blended.

2. Add the nuts and remove from the heat.

3. Quickly spoon the mixture into your mold and refrigerate until solid.

2 tablespoons vegan margarine or coconut oil

1 cup powdered sugar

Pinch salt

¼ cup cocoa powder

1 teaspoon vanilla extract

2 tablespoons non-dairy milk

2 tablespoons roughly chopped walnuts or almonds

Rustic Tarte Tatin

Puff pastry is ideal for creating fast desserts with minimal effort. Store-bought brands are almost always vegan (check the ingredients to confirm). They're ideal for two because you can slice off just as much or little as you need. Here, it forms the foundation for rustic apple tart.

PREP TIME:
10 MINUTES

COOK TIME:
20 MINUTES

1 apple, peeled, cored, and thinly sliced
1 teaspoon vegan margarine
1 tablespoon sugar
½ teaspoon ground cinnamon
2 tablespoons water
Pinch salt
1 sheet puff pastry, thawed and cut into two 3- by 5-inch rectangles (refreeze the remainders)

1. Preheat the oven to 400°F.

2. In a small saucepan over medium heat, add the apple slices, margarine, sugar, cinnamon, water, and salt. Simmer, covered, for 5 minutes, or until the apples are soft. Remove from the heat.

3. On a parchment-lined baking sheet, arrange the puff pastry sheets and top with the apple mixture.

4. Bake for 15 minutes, or until the dough has puffed up and the apples are golden.

5. Serve warm or cool.

PREP TIME:
15 MINUTES

COOK TIME:
15 MINUTES

Coco-Choco Macaroons

Coconut and chocolate are an indulgent pairing, and this pared-down recipe showcases their natural affinity. These macaroons freeze well, but odds are good that they won't last long enough for cold storage. Skip the chocolate chips if you're pinched for time; they taste divine without any adornment.

1. Preheat the oven to 350°F.

2. In a medium bowl, combine the coconut, flour, sugar, agave nectar, vanilla, salt, and 2 tablespoons milk to form a thick dough.

3. Using your hands, form the dough into six small balls.

4. On a parchment-lined baking sheet, gently place the macaroons, giving each a bit of breathing room. Bake for 10 minutes, then remove from the oven.

5. While the macaroons cool, place a heat-proof bowl over a small saucepan of simmering water. Add the chocolate chips and remaining 2 teaspoons non-dairy milk, stirring regularly until melted.

6. To serve, dip half of each macaroon in the chocolate and return to the parchment paper to cool before eating.

1 cup shredded coconut
2 tablespoons all-purpose
   flour
¼ cup sugar
2 teaspoons agave nectar
½ teaspoon vanilla extract
Pinch salt
2 tablespoons non-dairy milk,
   plus 2 teaspoons, divided
¼ cup dark chocolate chips

Raw Carrot Cake

Prep time for this raw dessert is just 5 minutes. The end result is not only decadent, but full of good-for-you ingredients that taste more indulgent than they really are. Dates are naturally very, very sweet, so if you prefer a less sugary treat, omit the powdered sugar in the frosting.

For the frosting
½ cup **Cashew Crème**
    (page 153)
1 tablespoon **powdered sugar**
Zest of ½ **lemon**

For the cake
2 **carrots**, shredded
    (about 1 cup)
6 **dates**, pitted
2 tablespoons roughly
    chopped **walnuts**
2 tablespoons **shredded
    coconut**
½ teaspoon **ground cinnamon**
1 teaspoon **vanilla**
Pinch **salt**

To make the frosting

In a small bowl, combine the cashew crème, powdered sugar, and lemon zest. Stir to combine.

To make the cake

1. In a food processor, pulse the carrots, dates, walnuts, coconut, cinnamon, vanilla, and salt until a thick dough is formed. Press the mixture into your mold of choice—a muffin tin with a strip of parchment paper works well—and refrigerate to firm up.

2. To serve, remove the mini cakes from their molds, plate, and top with frosting.

Magic Medjool Truffles

Medjool dates are the source of sweetness in these easy truffles. They're expensive, but worth it, and you'll only need 10 for this recipe. You can substitute easier-to-find and less expensive deglet noor dates, but the rich, caramel flavor won't be as pronounced.

1. In a food processor, pulse all the ingredients together to form a thick paste.

2. Roll into balls.

3. Roll in cocoa powder and refrigerate to firm up before serving.

10 medjool dates, pitted
2 tablespoons cocoa powder, plus extra for rolling
1 teaspoon coconut oil
½ teaspoon vanilla
Pinch salt

Banana Split Parfait

Reminiscent of an old-fashioned banana split, this layered dessert is served in a glass and topped with a drizzle of dark chocolate syrup. If it's berry season, swap out the bananas for strawberries or raspberries for a blast of color and tartness.

¼ cup dark chocolate chips

1 tablespoon non-dairy milk

1 cup Cashew Crème (page 153), blended with 1 tablespoon agave or powdered sugar

1 banana, thinly sliced

2 tablespoons roughly chopped toasted walnuts

Shredded coconut (optional)

1. Place a heat-proof bowl over a small saucepan of simmering water. Add the chocolate chips and non-dairy milk, stirring regularly until melted.

2. While the chocolate melts, spoon 1 tablespoon of the sweetened Cashew Crème into each glass. Top with a layer of banana, followed by another layer of crème. Repeat, finishing with a layer of crème.

3. Spoon the chocolate sauce over the top, add the nuts and coconut (if using). Serve immediately.

TIP: *Instead of Cashew Crème, try making this dessert with home-made coconut whipped cream. Chill a large can of coconut milk in the freezer for 20 minutes, then open and skim the thick layer of cream off the top. Using a hand mixer, beat until frothy and firm.*

PREP TIME:
10 MINUTES

Three-Step Tiramisu

A classic Italian dessert redolent of coffee and chocolate gets a modern makeover with the help of accidentally vegan Speculoos cookies. Like a parfait, this tiramisu is served in a glass, and can be chilled in the refrigerator before serving or devoured immediately.

1. Place a heat-proof bowl over a small saucepan of simmering water. Add the chocolate chips and non-dairy milk, stirring regularly until melted.

2. While the chocolate melts, spoon a heaping tablespoon of Speculoos cookies into each glass, followed by a teaspoon of coffee. Top with a teaspoon of chocolate chips and a large dollop of Cashew Crème. Repeat, finishing with Cashew Crème.

3. To serve, dust with cinnamon (if using).

TIP: *Speculoos have a lightly spiced, buttery flavor but are made from just a few, completely vegan ingredients. If you're lucky enough to find it near you, try the equally delicious—and equally vegan—Speculoos spread—which has the consistency of smooth peanut butter and can be used the same way.*

¼ cup dark chocolate chips

1 tablespoon non-dairy milk

10 Speculoos cookies, lightly crushed (about 1 cup)

2 tablespoons strong coffee, cooled

1 cup Cashew Crème (page 153), blended with 1 tablespoon agave or powdered sugar

Ground cinnamon, for dusting (optional)

Whoopee! Pies

Whoopie pies are typically stuffed with a supercharged cream center that's loaded with sugar and fat. This updated version offers the same cakey, creamy allure, but with a toned-down filling made with cashew crème. If you're not shouting "whoopee!" after your first bite, take another!

PREP TIME:
20 MINUTES

COOK TIME:
10 MINUTES

For the filling
½ cup Cashew Crème
(page 153)
1 tablespoon powdered sugar
Pinch ground cinnamon
(optional)

For the pie
1 cup all-purpose flour
½ cup cocoa powder
1 teaspoon baking soda
½ teaspoon baking powder
Pinch salt
½ cup non-dairy milk,
blended with 1 teaspoon
vinegar
1 teaspoon vanilla extract
2 tablespoons vegan
margarine
¼ cup sugar

To make the filling

In a small bowl, combine the Cashew Crème, sugar, and cinnamon. Refrigerate until ready to use.

To make the pie

1. Preheat the oven to 375°F.

2. In a large bowl, stir together the flour, cocoa powder, baking soda, baking powder, and salt.

3. In another large bowl, cream together the milk-vinegar mixture, vanilla, margarine, and sugar. Using a hand mixer or a whisk, beat until creamy. Add the dry ingredients and stir to combine.

4. On a parchment-lined baking sheet, scoop four heaping tablespoons of batter, leaving a few inches between each scoop. Bake for 10 minutes.

5. To serve, spread one cake slice with a generous spoonful of crème filling, and top with a second cake slice. Repeat for the second whoopee pie, and serve.

Amaretto Mousse

PREP TIME:
5 MINUTES

COOK TIME:
5 MINUTES

It's not a secret anymore: Avocados make great desserts. Here, the fruit is transformed into a creamy mousse, with nary a hint of avocado flavor to interfere with the chocolate-amaretto goodness. Substitute vanilla extract for the amaretto for a more subtle and traditional chocolate mousse flavor.

1. Place a heat-proof bowl over a small saucepan of simmering water. Add the chocolate chips and 1 tablespoon of the non-dairy milk, stirring regularly until melted.

2. In a food processor, combine the avocados, sugar, cocoa powder, remaining 3 tablespoons milk, almond extract, and salt. Blend until smooth and creamy. Spoon into glasses and refrigerate a minimum of 1 hour to set.

TIP: *Not all liqueurs are created equal: Some are not vegan! However, many are, including Italian Amaretto. Before buying your booze, do a search on Barnivore (barnivore.com) to confirm that your tipple is vegan-approved.*

¼ cup dark chocolate chips
¼ cup non-dairy milk, divided
2 ripe avocados, halved, pitted, and scooped from skins
2 tablespoons powdered sugar
¼ cup cocoa powder
1 teaspoon bitter almond extract or Amaretto liqueur
Pinch salt

Peanut Butter Cookies

Peanut butter is so rich all on its own that no extra oil is needed for this recipe. The cookies come out of the oven soft and chewy and firm up a bit as they cool; resist the temptation to eat them immediately—or to gobble up the batter before they even make it into the oven!

PREP TIME:
10 MINUTES

COOK TIME:
10 MINUTES

¼ cup peanut butter
¼ cup turbinado sugar
1 teaspoon vanilla extract
2 tablespoons non-dairy milk
3 tablespoons
    all-purpose flour
½ teaspoon baking soda
Pinch salt (omit if using salted
    peanut butter)

1. Preheat the oven to 375°F.

2. In a medium bowl, stir together the peanut butter, sugar, vanilla, and milk.

3. In a small bowl, combine the flour, baking soda, and salt. Add the flour mixture to the peanut butter mixture, and stir or knead to form a thick dough.

4. On a parchment-lined baking sheet, scoop four balls of dough, and flatten using a fork.

5. Bake for 10 minutes, or until the edges just begin to turn golden.

TIP: *Turn your peanut butter cookies into a tempting PB&J-style sandwich cookie by swirling a spoonful of your favorite jam into a tablespoonful of Cashew Crème (page 153), then spreading the mixture between two cookies. Cover with plastic wrap and let set in the freezer for 20 minutes before digging in.*

Mango & Raspberry Parfaits

This healthy dessert is crunchy, creamy, and full of bright fruit flavors. Use a really ripe mango for best results, and if you have fresh vanilla beans at your disposal, scrape the sweet-smelling pulp from one pod and use in place of the vanilla extract.

1. Using an immersion blender or standard blender, purée the mango pulp with the vanilla until smooth.

2. Spoon ⅛ cup granola into each parfait glass. Top with a heaping tablespoon of mango purée, then four or five raspberries. Top each serving with half the Cashew Crème, followed by a few more berries. The parfaits can be refrigerated before serving, but taste best when berries are at room temperature.

1 small, ripe mango, peeled, pitted, and sliced into chunks

½ teaspoon vanilla extract

¼ cup Nutty Olive Oil Granola (pg. 38)

¼ cup raspberries

½ cup Cashew Crème (page 153), blended with 1 tablespoon agave

Easiest Banana Ice Cream

SOY-FREE
NUT-FREE
QUICK & EASY

If you're trying this insanely easy recipe for the first time, it's normal to be slightly skeptical about just how satisfying something with so few ingredients can be. Of course, once you've actually tried it, you'll be among those who can't stop raving about it to friends and family.

PREP TIME:
5 MINUTES

3 bananas, frozen
¼ teaspoon vanilla extract
Pinch of salt

1. Slice the frozen bananas into 2-inch pieces.

2. In a food processor, add the frozen banana pieces and pulse. Once the bananas are pulverized, stop and scrape down the sides of the food processor.

3. Add the vanilla and salt, and begin pulsing again until you reach a smooth, ice cream–like texture.

TIP: *The only catch to this recipe is that your bananas have to be completely frozen for the texture to come out correctly. It is best to freeze them at least overnight before making this dish.*

BASICS & GO-TOS

PREP TIME:
10 MINUTES

COOK TIME:
20 MINUTES

Essential Marinara

You'll never buy marinara sauce again once you discover how easy it is to make yourself. The key ingredients—tomato, garlic, onions, and herbs—are all you need for a great foundation. To gussy your marinara up, add olives, mushrooms, peppers, or other vegetables, and enjoy on your pasta of choice.

1. In a medium nonstick skillet over medium heat, add the oil and onion. Sauté, stirring, for 4 minutes. Add the garlic and herbs. Sauté 2 minutes more.

2. Add the tomato paste, crushed tomatoes, wine, sugar, and salt. Simmer, stirring, for 15 minutes.

3. Serve warm over pasta.

TIP: *You can use fresh tomatoes or whole canned tomatoes in this recipe instead of crushed tomatoes; just chop finely or give a few whirs with an immersion blender to achieve the texture.*

1 tablespoon extra-virgin olive oil
1 small onion, finely chopped
2 garlic cloves
1 teaspoon dried Italian herbs (oregano, basil, parsley)
3 tablespoons tomato paste
1 (15-ounce) can crushed tomatoes
¼ cup red wine
1 teaspoon sugar (optional)
1 teaspoon salt

Spinach Pesto

SOY-FREE
GLUTEN-FREE
QUICK & EASY

PREP TIME:
10 MINUTES

Pesto is so easy to make at home, and can be whipped up in less than 5 minutes. This recipe calls for easy-to-find spinach and can be used exactly how you would the more common variety made with basil. For a more traditional flavor, substitute basil for half of the spinach.

4 cups roughly chopped spinach

2 garlic cloves, halved

2 tablespoons extra-virgin olive oil

2 tablespoons raw nuts (pine nuts, walnuts, almonds, or cashews)

2 tablespoons nutritional yeast

Combine all the ingredients in a food processor or blender and pulse until smooth. This pesto will keep for several days in the refrigerator. Drizzle with a little extra oil if you won't be eating it right away.

TOSS IT TOGETHER TIP: *Just a little pesto left in the jar? Add a bit of extra-virgin olive oil and vinegar, shake vigorously, and pour over salad greens for a bright blast of flavor.*

20-Minute Pizza Dough

Whether you like a deep dish–style pizza or the thin-crust variety, this is your recipe. It will yield one thick pizza crust or two thin crusts, but you could also turn it into dinner rolls or focaccia bread with the addition of a few herbs and spices.

PREP TIME:
30 MINUTES

COOK TIME:
20 MINUTES

1. In a medium bowl, add the yeast and sugar. Pour in the hot water and let sit for two minutes, or until the mixture begins to froth.

2. Add the salt and flour and mix until the dough becomes firm. Knead by hand in the bowl for 1 minute and shape into a soft ball.

3. In a large bowl, add the oil. Add the ball of dough and turn in the oil to coat.

4. Let the dough rise for 15 minutes, or until doubled in size, then punch down into another ball.

5. Press the dough into a lightly-oiled pizza pan. (For a thin crust, divide the dough into two balls.)

6. Preheat the oven to 450°F.

7. Add sauce and toppings of choice.

8. Bake on the middle rack of the oven for 20 minutes, or until the crust turns a golden brown.

1 tablespoon active dry yeast
1 teaspoon sugar
1 cup hot water
1 teaspoon salt
2 cups all-purpose flour
1 tablespoon extra-virgin olive oil

Cashew Crème

SOY-FREE
GLUTEN-FREE

PREP TIME:
5 MINUTES

Cashew nuts possess an inherent sweetness and a rich texture, which makes them perfect for transforming into a crème that can go savory with the right spices, or sweetened for use in homemade desserts. When stored in a clean glass jar in the refrigerator, it'll keep for up to a week. You'll need to soak the cashews ahead of time to keep this quick and easy.

1 cup raw cashews
2 cups water, for soaking,
  plus ¼ cup
Pinch salt

1. In a medium bowl, add the cashews and 2 cups water. Cover, and let soak for a minimum of 4 hours, or overnight.

2. Drain and rinse the cashews.

3. In a blender or food processor, add the cashews and salt. Blend, adding water as needed to reach a smooth and creamy consistency.

Tahini-Garlic Dressing

PREP TIME:
5 MINUTES

If you've ever tried bottled "goddess"-style dressing and loved the rich flavor, you'll want to put this dressing into regular rotation at mealtimes. Not only does it make a delectable salad dressing, but it also works as a sauce for rice, steamed veggies, and grilled tofu or tempeh.

1. In a small bowl, add the garlic, soy sauce, tahini, lemon juice, and herbes de Provence. Whisk together by hand or with an immersion blender. If the sauce is too thick, add a little water to thin.

2. Serve immediately or refrigerate until ready to use.

2 garlic cloves, minced

2 teaspoons soy sauce or wheat-free tamari

3 tablespoons tahini

Juice of ½ lemon

½ teaspoon herbes de Provence

Almond Parmesan

GLUTEN-FREE
QUICK & EASY
SOY-FREE

PREP TIME:
5 MINUTES

Store these cheese-like sprinkles in a container with a shaker top and use as a savory topping for popcorn, pasta, or pizza. To add a little more oomph, try experimenting with the addition of seasonings, such as chipotle powder or Italian herbs.

½ cup raw almonds or walnuts
1 tablespoon nutritional yeast
½ teaspoon garlic powder
½ teaspoon salt

1. In a food processor, add the almonds, nutritional yeast, garlic powder, and salt. Pulse until you reach a crumbly texture.

2. Store in a cool, dry place. The parmesan will stay fresh for up to a month.

Spicy Peanut Sauce

PREP TIME:
5 MINUTES

COOK TIME:
5 MINUTES

This versatile sauce draws on the flavors of Southeast Asian cuisine, and marries well with food from that corner of the world: fried noodles, satay, steamed rice. Let your imagination run with the possibilities, and enjoy the tasty experimentation process.

1. In a small saucepan over medium heat, add the garlic, ginger, peanut butter, coconut milk, soy sauce, lime juice, and red pepper flakes (if using).

2. Simmer, stirring, for 2 minutes.

3. Serve immediately.

2 garlic cloves, minced

½ inch piece fresh ginger, peeled and grated

3 tablespoons peanut butter

3 tablespoons coconut milk

2 teaspoons soy sauce or wheat-free tamari

Juice of ½ a lime

Pinch red pepper flakes (optional)

Mushroom Gravy

QUICK & EASY
SOY-FREE

PREP TIME:
5 MINUTES

COOK TIME:
15 MINUTES

Gravy is an indispensable holiday-meal tradition, and this recipe makes it easy for you to incorporate those warming, homey flavors into your cooking year-round. Use whatever mushrooms are available, and replace the red wine with non-dairy milk for a creamier version.

1 tablespoon extra-virgin olive oil
1 small onion, minced
1 garlic clove, minced
½ teaspoon dried sage
1 cup chopped mushrooms
1 tablespoon cornstarch, dissolved in 1 cup red wine
2 tablespoons nutritional yeast
1 teaspoon salt
Freshly ground black pepper
½ cup water

1. In a medium nonstick skillet over medium heat, add the oil and onions. Sauté, stirring, for 5 minutes, or until the onions are translucent and soft. Add the garlic and sage. Cook, stirring, for 2 minutes more.

2. Add the mushrooms and sauté for 3 minutes, or until the mushrooms release their juices and shrink by half.

3. Add the cornstarch-wine mixture and nutritional yeast. Simmer, stirring, until the mixture begins to thicken, about 3 minutes. Add the salt and season with pepper, adding water as necessary to thin the gravy.

4. Cook 2 minutes more, then serve.

TIP: *It's no secret that gravy is great over mashed potatoes, but there are endless uses for this liquid comfort food beyond the spud. Try it as a base for pot pies, a topping for breakfast biscuits, or a hearty sauce for baked potatoes.*

GLUTEN-FREE
SOY-FREE
NUT-FREE
QUICK & EASY

PREP TIME:
5 MINUTES

Infused Extra-Virgin Olive Oil

Extra-virgin olive oil is pretty amazing all on its own, but there's a simple way to turn this everyday staple into a special treat, and that's simply by adding herbs and spices and allowing the flavors to permeate the oil. Use a good-quality oil for the tastiest results.

1. In a clean, dry bottle, add the dried ingredients, followed by the oil.

2. Top with a pourable spout and let infuse for 24 hours before using.

3. Store in a cool, dry place.

TIP: *This oil can be used for cooking in the same way you'd use any extra-virgin olive oil, but its real appeal is its nuanced flavor poured straight out of the bottle. Drizzle it over fresh bread, garlic toast, and straight-out-of-the-oven pizza slices for something really special.*

¼ cup mixed dried herbs, dried chile peppers, dried lemon peel, peppercorns, or a combination

1 cup extra-virgin olive oil

Nacho "Cheese" Sauce

This sauce gets its cheesiness from an unexpected source: Potatoes. The same waxy variety that will turn your mashed potatoes into glue will yield a perfectly gooey sauce that's surprisingly cheese-like.

PREP TIME:
10 MINUTES

COOK TIME:
30 MINUTES

1 teaspoon extra-virgin olive oil

1 small onion, minced

1 garlic clove, minced

½ teaspoon ground cumin

2 teaspoons cornstarch, dissolved in 1 cup water

2 tablespoons nutritional yeast

½ teaspoon salt

2 small fingerling or waxy potatoes, peeled, roughly chopped, and steamed for 10 minutes

1 chipotle pepper in adobo sauce, seeded and minced

Juice of ½ lemon

1. In a medium saucepan over medium heat, add the oil and onion. Sauté, stirring, for 5 minutes.

2. Add the garlic and cumin. Cook 2 minutes more, and then add the cornstarch-water mixture. Simmer, stirring, for 5 minutes.

3. Add the nutritional yeast and salt. Simmer 5 minutes more, stirring occasionally.

4. Remove from the heat.

5. Add the potatoes, chipotle pepper, and lemon juice. Using an immersion or standard blender, purée until smooth and silky.

6. Return to the heat, and simmer gently 5 minutes before ladling over tortilla chips, steamed veggies, or pasta.

PREP TIME:
5 MINUTES

Herb Dressing

This vivid green dressing gets its alluring hue from fresh herbs, and its creamy texture from the wonderfully versatile avocado. Use it as a salad dressing or as a dip for crudités, and if possible, don't refrigerate, or it will lose some of its bright color and fresh flavor.

Using an immersion blender or standard blender, purée all the ingredients until smooth. If the dressing is too thick, thin with the juice from the remaining lemon half. Serve immediately.

1 ripe avocado, peeled, pitted, and sliced

1 garlic clove, minced

1 cup fresh herbs, such as dill, basil, or cilantro, washed and firmly packed

1 tablespoon olive oil

Juice of ½ lemon

Salt, to taste

Simple Vinaigrette

NUT-FREE
QUICK & EASY

PREP TIME:
5 MINUTES

On nights when all you really want is a simple salad, this dressing will elevate whatever fixin's you have on hand. This is a versatile base that's easily customizable with fresh or dried spices, so if you're partial to tarragon, oregano, or a mix like herbes de Provence, add them in to taste.

¼ cup olive oil
1 tablespoon Dijon mustard
1 tablespoon vegan mayonnaise
2 tablespoons Champagne vinegar or red wine vinegar
½ teaspoon maple syrup
1 garlic clove
Salt

Using an immersion blender or regular blender, combine all the ingredients until smooth. Serve immediately.

THE DIRTY DOZEN AND THE CLEAN 15

A nonprofit and environmental watchdog organization called Environmental Working Group (EWG) looks at data supplied by the U.S. Department of Agriculture (USDA) and the Food and Drug Administration (FDA) about pesticide residues and compiles a list each year of the best and worst pesticide loads found in commercial crops. You can use these lists to decide which fruits and vegetables to buy organic to minimize your exposure to pesticides and which produce is considered safe enough to skip the organics. This does not mean they are pesticide-free, though, so wash these fruits and vegetables thoroughly.

These lists change every year, so make sure you look up the most recent before you fill your shopping cart. You'll find the most recent lists as well as a guide to pesticides in produce at http://EWG.org/FoodNews.

The 2015 DIRTY DOZEN

- Apples
- Celery
- Cherry tomatoes
- Cucumbers
- Grapes
- Nectarines
- Peaches
- Potatoes
- Snap peas
- Spinach
- Strawberries
- Sweet bell peppers

Plus produce contaminated with highly toxic organophosphate insecticides:

- Hot peppers
- Kale/Collard greens

The CLEAN 15

- Asparagus
- Avocados
- Cabbage
- Cantaloupe
- Cauliflower
- Eggplant
- Grapefruit
- Kiwi
- Mangos
- Onions
- Papayas
- Pineapples
- Sweet corn
- Sweet peas (frozen)
- Sweet potatoes

MEASUREMENT CONVERSIONS

VOLUME EQUIVALENTS (LIQUID)

US STANDARD	US STANDARD (OUNCES)	METRIC (APPROXIMATE)
2 tablespoons	1 fl. oz.	30 mL
¼ cup	2 fl. oz.	60 mL
½ cup	4 fl. oz.	120 mL
1 cup	8 fl. oz.	240 mL
1½ cups	12 fl. oz.	355 mL
2 cups or 1 pint	16 fl. oz.	475 mL
4 cups or 1 quart	32 fl. oz.	1 L
1 gallon	128 fl. oz.	4 L

OVEN TEMPERATURES

FAHRENHEIT (F)	CELSIUS (C) (APPROXIMATE)
250	120
300	150
325	165
350	180
375	190
400	200
425	220
450	230

VOLUME EQUIVALENTS (DRY)

US STANDARD	METRIC (APPROXIMATE)
⅛ teaspoon	0.5 mL
¼ teaspoon	1 mL
½ teaspoon	2 mL
¾ teaspoon	4 mL
1 teaspoon	5 mL
1 tablespoon	15 mL
¼ cup	59 mL
⅓ cup	79 mL
½ cup	118 mL
⅔ cup	156 mL
¾ cup	177 mL
1 cup	235 mL
2 cups or 1 pint	475 mL
3 cups	700 mL
4 cups or 1 quart	1 L
½ gallon	2 L
1 gallon	4 L

WEIGHT EQUIVALENTS

US STANDARD	METRIC (APPROXIMATE)
½ ounce	15 g
1 ounce	30 g
2 ounces	60 g
4 ounces	115 g
8 ounces	225 g
12 ounces	340 g
16 ounces or 1 pound	455 g

RESOURCES

After you've filled your pantry full of vegan staples, you'll want to stock up on a few other items to help bring ease, convenience, and fun to the cooking process. These books and e-resources will guide you through any potential stumbling blocks, and support you long after you've mastered the kitchen crafts.

Books

Plant Power by Nava Atlas

How to Be Vegan by Elizabeth Castoria

Chloe's Vegan Desserts by Chloe Coscarelli

Isa Does It by Isa Chandra Moskowitz

Vegan Without Borders by Robin Robertson

Salad Samurai by Terry Hope Romero

Websites

Chocolate Covered Katie
http://chocolatecoveredkatie.com

Fat Free Vegan Kitchen
http://blog.fatfreevegan.com

The Joyful Vegan
www.joyfulvegan.com

Oh She Glows
http://ohsheglows.com

The Post Punk Kitchen
www.theppk.com

Vegan Richa
www.veganricha.com

VegWeb
http://vegweb.com

YouTube Channels

Everyday Dish TV
www.youtube.com/user/everydaydish

Jason Wrobel
www.youtube.com/user/JasonWrobelTV

The Sexy Vegan
www.youtube.com/user/lukin82

Vegan Cooking With Love
www.youtube.com/user/VeganCookingWithLove

The Vegan Zombie
www.youtube.com/user/ZombieGate

Apps

HappyCow

Is It Vegan?

Kitchen Calculator Pro

Vegan Nom Nom

INDEX

CPSIA information can be obtained
at www.ICGtesting.com
Printed in the USA
BVOW10s1725090717
488257BV00002B/2/P